Now What?

Notes From the Front Lines of Old Age

Sandra Butler

This is a work of nonfiction. However, certain names and details of the characters' lives and physical appearances have been changed, and some events have been altered or combined for the sake of narrative continuity. The author in no way represents any company, corporation, or brand, mentioned herein. The views expressed in this memoir are solely those of the author and do not represent the views of the publisher.

Rattling Good Yarns Press
33490 Date Palm Drive 3065
Cathedral City CA 92235
USA
www.rattlinggoodyarns.com

Cover Design: Rattling Good Yarns Press

Library of Congress Control Number: 2026931660
ISBN: 978-1-955826-98-3

First Edition

This one is for Nan

visionary

supporter

challenger

guide

and beloved friend.

Contents

"Old age is an excellent time for outrage. My goal is
to say or do at least one outrageous thing every
week."
—Maggie Kuhn, founder of the Gray Panthers

"There are years that ask questions and years that
answer"
—Zora Neale Hurston

Introduction

I began to record my aging when I turned 80. *I wrote The Kitchen is Closed: And Other Benefits of Being Old*, then *Leaving Home at 83*, and now the book you're holding—or reading on a screen. I'm 87 now and want to begin *Now What?* by giving you a sense of first how—and then why—it has felt essential for me to write about these years.

As a child, stories about people's lives entered my eager ears through the glowing bulbs in the back of a 1944 white Crosley radio on the night table beside my bed. I escaped to my bedroom after dinner as quickly as I could, got ready for bed long before I needed to, and settled on my pillow, reached over to turn on the radio, turned off the lights, and let the words wash over me. I spent thousands of hours listening in the quiet, learning how other people lived, eager for the interactions of ordinary daily life, sounds absent in my house.

At night, I'd lie in bed looking at the spines of my books neatly lined up in my white bookcase and imagine my friends asleep inside their pages. Even now, the sign of a spine can bring the book in its entirety back to me, a threshold to a world the author created.

I devoured books, indiscriminately, passionately, urgently apprenticing myself to language that transported me to worlds of mystery, of love, of connection. There was always a stack of ten books on my bedside table, the maximum the librarian would allow students to check out at one time, each new book a doorway to a world I was eager to enter, leaving my own behind.

The stories I read myself led directly to my own attempts to create my own. I began to speak in the pages of my diary, recording a hidden life in a hidden book. The blank pages received and held my hesitant words, revealing in great detail what it was to be me. Then, such confessions were intended to be private. Only much later did I begin to understand the value of describing and defining my life in public. I learned that if I didn't use my own words to describe what it was to be me and what I saw in the world around me through my own eyes, the descriptions of me and of my world wouldn't be the truth of things.

Seven years ago, I squared my spindly shoulders and entered my 80s. I was sure I knew what to expect, given that I had lived through my 70s, but I quickly realized I had almost no idea what this decade would require of me. In a discomforting echo of how my 60s didn't prepare me for the complexities of my 70s, I soon found myself in unfamiliar and increasingly demanding terrain. I was still me, of course, and relievedly most of the time, that came in handy. But what used to be the case was becoming irrelevant, immaterial, and often entirely beside the point.

I did what I have always done when trying to make sense of something I don't yet understand: I wrote about it. *The Kitchen is Closed: And Other Benefits of Being Old* was my discovery and exploration of what being old means to others and what it represented for me. I wrote about the limitations of aging bodies. The freedom to release all the responsibilities that shaped the earlier decades of our lives. The tender foolishness of worrying that our car keys may be in the freezer. (They never are.) The proper nouns that continue to disappear. The freedom to no longer care about the things that once mattered so desperately. The pleasures of our own company. The truth about us. Funny. Bawdy. Vulnerable. Fearful. Ridiculous (that's where my pedicures come in.) *Kitchen* was an invaluable record, illuminating those early beginnings of my 80s.

Three years later, the second book, *Leaving Home at 83*, was my account of a massive rupture—the story of my impulsive and fearful self-exile from my community and fifty-year life in the San Francisco Bay Area. Wanting a way to live closer to my daughters, I moved into what my mother would have scornfully called a "place" in Phoenix.

Those years required me to confront the fading struggle to sustain my autonomy. The growing, conflicted longing to be taken care of, as I grew more vulnerable, was something I disapproved of in myself and had fought against all my life. Both longings were embedded in my desire "not to be a burden to those I love." Familiar?

Now What? Notes From the Front Lines of Old Age is my third book about living while old. I'm closer to 90 than 80 now and am happily settled into an independent (so far) life in Tucson that works for me. My understanding of life in the old and slow lane has deepened as I've made my way through this decade, and in Now What, I want to incorporate more of who

I was before I got old and how I'm living those identities now. All of my current publicity materials describe me this way:

Old. Jewish. Queer: All the rest is commentary.

One-word descriptors now feel insufficient and merely suggestive. To illuminate the richness of the identities that have shaped and defined my life, I turn to the framework of a spaghetti western—the good, the bad, and the ugly—well, perhaps if not ugly, at least some less-than-attractive truths from the front lines of my old age.

I live in an America that requires more of me as a lesbian and a Jew than I had anticipated, and these realities shape my old life. My mothering involves more lying to my lovingly overprotective daughters. My friends are dying, moving to be near children and restarting their lives, caring for sick partners, and being sick themselves. We're all a big, loving mess.

Very little is what I had expected, but that's been true of the entire decade so far. I still awaken intending to seize the day, but the news, or my knee, or not having enough milk for that first, critical cup of coffee can leave me without the focus required for sustained seizing. Being a writer, an activist, an old Jewish Queer, a mother to two middle-aged daughters, and a part of a far-flung community of women all require my full attention. I'm at the end of things and need to extract all the juice I can out of every one of these days.

Extreme oldness offers unexpected opportunities as well. I've finally won my lifelong battle to close a book I'm not enjoying or understanding, especially if it's one by a literary figure considered extremely deep, subtle, and avant-garde. I've had a lifelong struggle to understand avant-garde writing and am never entirely sure what the author is trying to get at. Now, if I'm not drawn in by the fiftieth page, that's it. But only after glancing at the last couple of pages to see where the story was headed and ultimately went. I'm no longer concerned with the potentially hurt feelings of the absent, albeit famous, author.

I say 'no thank you' more often. I soften the no with a thank you because I am my mother's child. Still, the no's come more easily than they once did. Sometimes I add a mini lie to the no. I don't like to drive at night. Or in the rain. Or because of the noise level in restaurants, the crowds at lectures and performances, the darkness in winter, and the heat in summer. I can always find something to add to my 'no' so that I'm left making only the choices I want to, and not hurting anyone's feelings. What's left are the yeses. It feels like freedom. (Thank you, Jon Batiste)

A heads up: there is not a single bit of uplift, and no suggestions about self-improvement discreetly nestled into these chapters. I don't know how you should live, feel, or think; I have no big life lessons to offer, nor any crone-like sagacity. I suspect you're just fine as you are. After all, you've been yourself for a long time.

In these pages, I offer some of the reflections that remain after a life in which I invited the stories of women, wrote about them, and lived long enough to uncover and reveal my own stories that had been hiding in plain sight. This is some of who I am right now—a glimpse that I hope will lead you to recognize something of yourself as well. And maybe consider forming a circle with other old women to talk everything over. Welcome.

Part One
Beginning—Yet Again

One
Beginning—Yet Again

In the space of eleven chaotic months, I had left my home of fifty years after a health scare, moved into a retirement community to be closer to my daughters, left there after nine unsuccessful months, and landed with a thump in Tucson, fragile, vulnerable, and scared.

Everything in my apartment was brand new; the original building had been a Benedictine monastery, now transformed into an upscale apartment complex after the aging sisters returned to their Mother House in the Midwest. It was the newness that captured me. I wanted to be new, to begin again.

There was a market, a library, a drugstore, and an art theater, all within walking distance. I felt a guarded optimism, along with a continuing sense of displacement and a stubborn determination, intermittently interrupted by bouts of weeping.

By the end of my first week, boxes had been emptied, broken down, and put outside. Dishes were neatly stacked in the cabinets, clothes were folded in drawers and hung on hangers, and shoes were lined up on the closet floor. My books filled the bookcases lining the wall in my study, with my current choices piled next to my bed in the order I intended to read them. Along with milk, coffee, bread, and other essentials, I bought fresh flowers, arranged them carefully in a vase I had bought in Jerusalem, and put them in the center of my freshly polished coffee table.

Since I was beginning this last chapter of my life in July, which for the uninitiated means months of three-digit heat, exploring Tucson would have to be put on hold until the summer ended. I would begin in an air-conditioned cocoon where all human contact would be navigated on Zoom. I could do this. I had to do this. Tucson was the last stop on this train.

I was the oldest resident of the Benedictine, like everybody's grandmother. As a result, I was either invisible to these sturdy young people or besieged with unnecessary offers to hold the door or carry packages, as though my gray hair and wrinkles required their physical attention. I'd smile warmly and demur, although I suspect there will be a time in the not-too-distant future when I'll be grateful for their kind assumptions of my inability to fetch and carry.

One of the selling points of my decision to move into a residential community in Phoenix was that I would be fed three meals a day. I always disliked cooking and was never very good at it. After I had provided meals for my daughters with sufficient skill and incorporation of all the food groups, so that they left home as well-nourished young adults, I ate in cafes and found the best-prepared soups and salads, takeout Indian and Chinese food, and rotisserie chicken available. I ate anything I didn't have to cook myself.

Now, I had a spacious, sleek, modern, white, and brushed-silver kitchen with an abundance of pantry space, so I determined to fill it up with a respectable range of supplies. I decided to launch my new kitchen, not by whacking a bottle of champagne against the refrigerator (which had crossed my mind), but by cooking a T-bone steak. It would be a treat since I ate very little red meat, and I would return to the pleasures, few though they are, of cooking. That is, until the fire engines arrived.

Off I went to a well-reviewed butcher to get a steak. If I were going to eat meat, it would be the best quality—my body a temple and all that. The next afternoon, as my upcoming feast was transitioning from the refrigerator to room temperature, I began my preparations, gathering the ingredients with the same attention given to a rarely practiced ritual.

I placed my cast-iron skillet in the oven to heat until it reached the necessary 400 degrees. Leaving the oven on, I removed the skillet and put it on high on the electric oven top. Into it went side one of a gorgeous oiled, salted, peppered steak for the first sear. My kitchen was filled with the glorious smell of cooking meat. After exactly the correct number of minutes (I looked it up), I turned the steak over, already anticipating the meal that awaited me. A meal consisting entirely of steak. Why gild a lily?

But now the smell was accompanied by smoke. The vent fan I had turned on didn't even make a dent in the clouds that were forming and enveloping the kitchen. I opened the patio door and aimlessly waved my arms around as if to invite the smoke to move in the direction of the outdoors, but within minutes, the smoke detectors went off. Everywhere in my wing of the complex. Populated by my very young neighbors.

I was now the object of my once dismissive assumptions about the kind of people who set off alarms. When I was still merely sixty and living in the apartment in California that had been my home for twenty-four years, the alarm went off at least once a month, nearly always at dinner time. The stairwells became clogged with disgruntled tenants following the recorded booming instructions to leave the building. The fire trucks arrived, and groups of people whispered about what they were certain was going on and who was undoubtedly at the root of it all. Within a half hour of milling around, we were given the all-clear and re-entered the building.

Whenever there was a cluster of such alarms, several in a week or two, the responsible old person was moved by their worried children to a residential facility where kitchens were no longer a part of their lives. We all, the younger residents, I mean, looked at each other and shrugged. Another kitchen fire. Nothing to be worried about. Old, confused, and ready to move to the next stage of life, people set off fire alarms. Not us.

Now, my alarm continued to clang as I held my breath, staring at the sprinklers in the ceiling, silently pleading with them not to do anything. If they had, my apartment would have been entirely flooded by the time the firefighters arrived. Those prayers were answered, but the alarm continued its insistent ringing through the hallways. I opened the front door, looked down the corridor, and was met with a half dozen faces peering out of their doors. Taking a deep breath, I stepped out in my caftan and slippers to let them know that all was well. It was just me searing some meat. I ducked back inside, not wanting to see the expressions on their faces and feel any more humiliated than I already was.

We exited the building; the most cavalier took the elevators, while everyone else clattered down the stairs, with me alternating between remorseful smiles and an averted gaze. I had become that old woman now—the one who was not to be trusted with a stove. Any efforts at redirecting my embarrassment by blaming the poor quality of the hood's ventilation system wouldn't give me any traction against my sense of mortification. That's one, I thought. Two more, and it's assisted living for me. Going forward, I may gently sauté a chicken breast or a piece of salmon, but the cast-iron pans are permanently out of service.

After several days had passed, an interval during which I hoped the young people had forgotten what I looked like and had returned to more interesting concerns than remembering the face of an old woman known to burn her food and set off fire alarms, my youngest daughter Ally called to tell me she had researched a local LGBTQ organization for oldies called Senior Pride and suggested I go to a gathering they offered the following Wednesday. It was advertised as Gayme Day, which resulted in my firm and unequivocal no.

"Why?" she persisted; my child was nothing if not persistent when it came to me.

"Because, you know, I don't play games. I don't like games. I'm not a player. I'm a talker," I said with a crankiness she ignored.

"Mom," she said, her voice dropping into the register that let me know she was serious, "You have to start somewhere. Just go."

I felt like a recalcitrant first grader, not wanting to peek out of the safety of my apartment and make my way into the world of other kids. I was disappointed in myself for being so timid, and after a big, noisy exhale designed to convey my irritated resignation, I said, 'Okay.'

The following week, I cautiously entered an institutional room at Habitat for Humanity, where the ga(y)mes were to be played, and was immediately confronted with a sea of rainbow flags, buttons, handouts, brochures, and men. Masked men; I was already here; I couldn't turn around and pretend I was looking for another group; there was no other group. This was it.

I smiled broadly, which was pointless since masks were still required at all gatherings. We were all old, of course. I mean, senior. The biggest of the masked men leaned forward and boomed,

"Welcome!"

I was surprised by the tears that threatened to surface at the sound of that word. Welcome. I was being welcomed. Even though I didn't play games, didn't call myself a senior, and hated wearing a mask, I was welcome. The first grader in me grew confident.

After introducing myself, I was directed to one of the four tables, where I had a choice of board games. Already seated were a lesbian couple (I could tell because they were wearing matching pastel tracksuits) and two men who looked as shy as I felt. After Geron, the big welcome guy, introduced himself, explained the mission of Senior Pride, and described the delights that awaited us at Gayme day, we were left to our own devices, which thankfully didn't result in our playing a game. The other three tables followed instructions, but we appeared to be a bunch of outliers who wanted to talk to each other. We even decided to take off our masks since we unmedically determined we were sitting far enough apart.

Our conversations followed two predictable but enjoyable tracks. What in our lives had led us to settle in Tucson, and how and when did we come out? Put any group of homosexuals together, and you can be pretty sure things will start there. And I love coming-out stories. I was up to at least junior high in my adventurousness by the end of the gathering.

After my first success, I returned to the Senior Pride website, searching for non-game events, and found the Book Club. It was to be on Zoom, but still, homosexuals talking about books was my idea of a promising opportunity, and the book they were discussing was one I'd already intended to read. I signed up and immersed myself with literary rigor akin to preparing for a final exam. I wanted to be ready.

Wearing my best Zoom-ready T-shirt, I watched as the squares filled up with the bookish members of Senior Pride. Everyone said hello and welcomed me before we settled into the discussion. I was in my element. Talking about structure, form, language, storytelling, character development, and themes—this was my kind of conversation. Everyone listened attentively to the member speaking, and no one interrupted, took up too much space, or was self-important—all behaviors that had been unsatisfying aspects of many of the book clubs I had been a part of in the past.

A woman two squares to my right responded to the text in a startling, wonderfully improvisational way. I took a deep breath, then direct messaged her saying I liked (first I wrote love, then deleted it because I didn't want to come on too strong and be misunderstood in my first effort to make a new friend); what she had said, and wondered if she'd like to meet for coffee. She did. The door of my new life swung open. In a stroke of my very good luck, Penelope was a woman deeply connected to the arts, writing, and lesbian communities in Tucson. She was the perfect guide to lead me into this desert neighborhood.

And lead me, she did. After a few coffee dates, she told me that a friend with whom she had been in a writing group had written a book about a Jewish woman fleeing a pogrom and creating a new life in New York. Did I want to go with her to the book launch at the Holocaust Museum? Did I? Was she kidding? Within weeks, the three of us decided to form a writing group. Each of us sought the impetus to meet and be accountable to one another as we worked on our current book project, which, for me, was an account of the last nine months in a residential facility, and became *Leaving Home at 83*.

I was growing more confident, increasingly able to drive to most places without my GPS, and ready to branch out. I went to a Senior Pride potluck, which wasn't my favorite form of socializing because of the not liking to cook thing, the inevitable too-high noise level, and not knowing who I was sitting next to. But the gods (goddesses) were with me, and I met Nancy. After several backyard visits (hers), she told me that her book group was opening up for new members and asked if I was interested. Two book groups? That was twice as good as one. Her group didn't solely read books by Ls, Gs, Bs, or Ts; the range of titles was broader and included literary fiction—my favorite. There I met lesbians with whom I connected easily, and I was off to the metaphoric races.

Penelope offered writing classes for Senior Pride members. I met Joyce there, and within a few weeks, her partner, Lavina, who had revived, and continued to maintain the ongoing visionary presence of Senior Pride. Then there were all the men. I hadn't interacted with so many gay men since San Francisco in the 1980s during the AIDS epidemic, but they were a part of Gay Pride and my life now. These were retired, aging men, not the enraged and terrified young men caught up in an epidemic I had known. They seemed quieter. Calmer. Older.

Within a few months, the Tucson Book Festival, a destination event for writers, booksellers, publicists, and readers, where nationally recognized writers gave talks, participated in panels, offered workshops, and were enthusiastically celebrated, invited local authors to submit their books to be chosen for a choice slot at one of the outdoor booths. I submitted *The Kitchen is Closed: And Other Benefits of Being Old,* the book I had written during the pandemic, which had been published a few months before I left Phoenix—and it was chosen!

I was given a three-hour window to display my book in a pavilion dedicated to indie writers before the next shift of authors would take over our coveted space. Long picnic tables formed a large square upon which each author was allotted three feet. I quickly grabbed a seat facing the central walkway and plopped my pile of books down. After my preemptive grab for the best spot, I turned and smiled broadly at everyone nearby, so I didn't look like a complete jerk—just a moderate one.

Everyone had brought colorful tablecloths and eye-catching merchandise to stand out from the other authors and attract the attention of the crowds of people moving through the multiple displays and pavilions. I hadn't considered a tablecloth; actually, I never consider tablecloths and no longer own one. Instead, I had created a large easel board with the book title, my picture, and the words:

OLD. JEWISH. QUEER. ALL THE REST IS
COMMENTARY.

Then I sat down behind the table and waited to see who that might bring my way. At first, people passed my literary offering, looking at me, trying to confirm if I was indeed queer since I had no immediately visible markers of queerness. Old, I already looked like. Jewish, perhaps to other Jews, but not necessarily. After making several tentative approaches, people began to approach my table, where the best part of the whole experience began.

I was given the gift of their stories; old women reminiscing about their own personal back-in-the-day, young ones marveling that I was 84 and still walking and talking and being a lesbian, buying books for their mothers and aunties, tightly held women wondering what it's like to write a book when I knew they were asking another, deeper question. What was it like to live my life out loud? There were dozens of women, eager, shy, curious—each offering their history to this stranger sitting by an easel that pronounced herself as Old. And Jewish. And Queer. The three hours raced by. Books were sold, cards were exchanged, and invitations were offered. And Senior Pride chose my book for their December Book Club meeting!

I was delighted to have my collection of essays serve as my introduction to this new community, and my date book was beginning to fill up with coffee and lunch dates. I still use a paper calendar, as I have always done. I tried putting my life into the phone, but first one daughter wanted to share her electronic calendar with me, while the other suggested we dovetail our appointment calendars in Google Docs. It was then I stopped using my phone for appointments. I simply couldn't keep up.

Penelope invited me to a poetry reading in a small alternative community started by academic hippies in the 1960s. We gathered in what was once a barn to listen to three gifted poets read from their latest collections. I was finding my way. Finding my people. A world was taking shape around me, one that had space for me. All of me. My nine months of institutional living were evaporating in the rearview mirror like a mirage.

I'm one of the oldest Senior Pride-ers. Most are younger in their senior-ness; some were parents before coming out and are now grandparents. Some have a religious practice, others are secular. We are culturally diverse, in various states of health and resources, and have, by now, all lost loved ones. For some of us, many beloveds. All that comes with the territory of aging.

As my connections in Senior Pride were unfolding and deepening, I began to explore the local resources that might provide a home for my Jewish religious and spiritual life. My spiritual teacher in the Bay Area, Jhos, and his wife, Julie, both service leaders, had encouraged and nourished my study and practice for decades, leading services with grace and wisdom, but had since moved on from congregational leadership. I knew enough to understand that looking back over my shoulder and comparing what might be available to me now with what I had been blessed to receive from them then would only make this transition more complicated. And like Lot's wife (nameless, of course), I'd turn into a pillar of salt.

I was here. My life was here, and I was going to have to figure out the Jewish part. It would have to be on Zoom because I couldn't manage masked. Never mind praying while masked. It was all I could do to breathe while masked.

The primary obstacle in this process was my judge-y comparativeness. I inherited it honestly from my mother, who had turned it into an art form. Still, for the past thirty years, I had done everything I could to rid myself of that vestige of her legacy. Every Tashlich, I threw it into the water, but when I returned home, or in some successful years, not till the next morning, there it was—back again. Being here now, as Ram Dass and all my Buddhist friends encourage, has worked when here is someplace I want to be, and I happily sink into where I am. Being in this here and now was going to require my best self.

A small rabbi-centered congregation co-sponsored an in-person event with Senior Pride focused on comparing vegetarian chopped liver recipes. As someone who isn't even crazy about regular chopped liver, I decided to stick my spiritual nose into the gathering to scope out the congregation and meet some Jews in addition to learning how (and why) people make vegetarian chopped liver at all.

The room was full of Jewish lesbians. Well, not all the way full, but the last couple of presidents of the congregation had been lesbians. This was promising. I made my way around the room, talking to the congregational members who were generous and engaging, and began to feel a sense of anticipatory excitement. Maybe this would be easier than I thought.

There were two long tables set up parallel to each other, with Senior Pride-ers at one and Jewish congregants at the other. I sat with the Jews, not the homosexuals. I already knew them.

The four competing vegan chopped liver platters were displayed at the front of the room, surrounded by lettuce and cherry tomatoes, to augment the visual appeal of an ice cream scoop of an artificial beige mound. At the given signal, people sitting at each table took turns going up to the front, gathering a paper plate, plastic spoon, and fork, and taking a small scoop of each of the offerings. We returned to our chairs and, after a thorough culinary dissection of the distinct qualities of each, a startling ability to identify seasonings and strong points of view about texture, to which I contributed exactly nothing, we voted for our favorites. While I consider myself someone with a reasonably well-developed palate, they all tasted pretty much the same, were medium brown, and had a similar consistency. I randomly selected a number, voted for it, and submitted my card.

The winner received energetic and appreciative applause and was thrilled to have her *balabusta* skills publicly confirmed. I began to move around the room, introducing myself as a new arrival, learning about the congregation and the lives of the chopped liver voters.

This was a Reform congregation, the denomination in which I had been brought up, the one I had left behind sixty years ago. I'd been a Renewal Jew for decades, a member of the first LGBT synagogue in the Bay Area, and then joined Chochmat Ha Lev, one of the first congregations centered on Jewish meditation. Being a part of a Reform synagogue, even one with a lot of lesbians, left me, as Adrienne Rich had long ago written, 'split at the root.'

I'd have to keep looking.

Two
Stepping

When the summer heat mercifully began to drop to temperatures that allowed me to be briefly outside in the early mornings and evenings, I began to step. I count each step, which was once called walking.

Twenty-five years ago, at a meeting of my women's group, each of us described the parts of our bodies we most prized. Mine was my stride. Breasts and widow's peaks, green eyes, and curly hair are all fine, but I'm tall, have long legs, and always loved the feeling of my legs swinging out from under me as I moved through the world. That was then. Now is quite a different matter.

I googled my age and gender to determine how many steps I needed to remain healthy. Between six and seven thousand steps, all the relevant sites urge. Enthusiastically. They were encouraging and supportive, reassuring me that I'd enjoy the outdoors (still a few months away), my digestive system would settle, my skin would glow, my heart would beat happily, and my lungs would fill me with fresh, clean air. How hard could it be to walk that far?

In my forties and fifties, I met friends for early morning walks in the still-foggy California redwoods. Some of the paths were quite steep, and as our years accumulated, we downshifted to less daunting trails. We walked and visited, breathing in the spicy scent of the trees, not counting our steps. We were just walking. Now, I can't climb hills, hike long distances, or even talk and walk at the same time because of the breathlessness that was one result of my lung surgery. Breathe or speak. I have to choose.

In the heat of the summer, when it doesn't matter what time you go out to walk, I tried what many Tucsonans do. I went to the mall that opened early so old people might march around before the shoppers descended. Once. I disapprove of malls, both the pricey ones and the working-class ones. They feel soulless and bloodless, filled with superfluous things made by children thousands of miles away that will dissolve upon washing or break upon even the slightest impact. And all those mom-and-pop stores that have been put out of business. Malls are just not for me.

One morning before dawn, instead of returning to bed after getting up to pee, I considered that, without any firsthand experience of fresh air in weeks, I'd get dressed and go outside to walk around the building. I wasn't sure how safe it would be, given that it was still dark out, but I was game.

Like the snorkeling experiences of my younger life when a world of sea creatures appeared just a few feet under the water, the streets were alive with grown-ups and children playing, people walking dogs, and women visiting in the dark. Pre-dawn walks were a splendid adaptation, I decided, and one I would fold into my routine. Not every morning, because who wants to get up at 4:45? But enough that I can breathe non-air-conditioned air a couple of times a week.

My alternative option to rising at dawn had been going to the gym in the building complex where there are treadmills and a range of mysterious machines designed to improve every part of my musculature. The problem is that my musculature had been at rest for decades; any improvement would be very minor and would only be considered when the gym is empty.

Sitting on a padded bench in the middle of the room and moving the weights down from 200 to 20 to get a couple of upper arm stretches under my belt is best done without witnesses. I've gone early in the morning, late in the evening, even at midday when everyone ought to be at work—but aren't. Someone is nearly always improving themselves, accompanied by grunts and swipes across their foreheads, spattering their self-congratulatory sweat everywhere.

I remain on the treadmill, safely tucked out of the line of machinery. Sometimes, I can grab a stretch or two if the gym is empty for twenty minutes. Still, mostly, I walk at a 3.0 level for half an hour, then pause when I sit down and drink water, and then return for fifteen minutes. That's as of this writing, anyway. When you read this, the time will undoubtedly be significantly shorter. I'm just showing off here.

I prop up my iPad and read a non-demanding mystery as I walk. The central plot propels the story forward, and time passes quickly. Listening to political podcasts while gazing at a TV screen playing excerpts of sporting events is not motivating. So, mysteries it is. When there are people on either side of me, they are wearing earphones, listening to music, or watching a movie on their phones (!!) and have no awareness that anyone else is inhabiting their space. We ignore one another.

Finally, summer wound down, and I was able to move outside. This required further preparation and the accumulation of the essential supplies needed for purposeful walking. I have a small collection of sneakers —white for summer and black and grey for winter, what's left of my old-school fashion statements in the shoe department. I know that's not a thing these days; sneakers come in all colors and designs that have nothing to do with seasons, but I was raised with the inflexible expectation that the articles of clothing I put on my body had some relationship to one another.

The company of interesting podcasts has replaced all my years of walking with interesting women. I switch back and forth between conversations, analyzing this political moment, and interviews with authors and reviewers about current fiction and poetry. I've been toggling between these subject matters all my life, long before there were such things as podcasts.

I put in my earbuds, the kind that attach to the phone with a wire, because my Bluetooth equipment kept falling out of my ears and rolling under things, requiring me to get on my hands and knees on the floor to look for them. I'd find them quickly enough, but the issue was getting up from the floor. Fully wired, sneakered, with a podcast cued up, there was still one final essential. I live in the desert, and when going out, for any reason and for any length of time, it is always necessary to carry a substantial bottle of water.

My Thermoflask Stainless Steel water bottle (my fourth because I keep leaving them behind in cafés and shops, like Gretel's breadcrumbs in the forest) has become an extension of my left hand whenever I go outside. The need to pay attention to my water absorption became clear after two days of feeling sick and aching from my hair follicles to my toes; I went to see my geriatrician and was quickly diagnosed as being massively dehydrated. That's all there was to it. Nothing was wrong. But it was massive. And felt really lousy.

All the experts caution—sternly—to consume half your body weight in daily ounces. Every. Single. Day. Which for me means eighty-eight interminable ounces! Coffee doesn't count. In fact, coffee was the opposite of a healthy drink, requiring me to add a glass of water to every cup I consumed. According to Google, coffee can also lead to a dull complexion, skin dryness, and eyes that appear sunken, none of which appeal to me as a way to look. To further complicate matters, I also found Google sites that assured me that coffee was considered an acceptable fluid. Apparently, I was to be left to my own caffeine-related devices. I split the difference and drank a massive mug first thing in the morning, and unless the day required a renewed jolt of energy, that was that.

I bought a pitcher with an infusion tube, allowing the addition of strawberries, basil, or mint to flavor the water and make all that determined drinking more motivating. My steps are currently accompanied by the omnipresent bottle of water, accompanied by a sprig of mint, basil, or a slice of orange or cucumber to keep things interesting.

I've committed myself to fully participating in my hydrated well-being, even reading the wellness columns in The New York Times to educate myself about supplements, a subject I have never fully understood. Some are good. Others are not. Some substances are excreted from your body if you have too much. Others build up, causing who knows what. Over the years, I've gone into health food stores and asked the person behind the counter what they recommend and why. I intend to sound like an informed consumer, even though I often struggle to understand their explanations and suspect they are recommending the most expensive choice. Plus, those places smell funny.

Earbuds in, sneakers on, Apple watch and phone programmed, water bottle filled, all that's left is sunscreen and a hat. I bought hats with big brims in various colors, but I'm still stuck in the "going with what I'm wearing" thing. Sometimes, I add a battery-operated fan hanging on a cord around my neck, designed to blow cool air into my face. The device works fine for about ten minutes, but when the cool air meets the hot air surrounding me, I receive blasts of lukewarm air. Undoubtedly, the reason for this was taught in one of the many high school classes I wasn't paying attention to.

There are no redwoods in the desert, and no sense of being enveloped in the trees. Instead, these days I walk on wide sun-drenched streets, passing homes purposefully landscaped with various cacti, stones, and some examples of southwest whimsy. At least, I think that's the intention. My knowledge of gardening decor doesn't extend very far.

I'm grateful that I live in a neighborhood with flat streets, where the only inclines are the occasional speed bumps. Walking to the first traffic light from my building and back allows me to accumulate 3,500 steps. Getting to the second light and back gets me to my step goal. Still, that precludes the possibility of doing anything else for the remainder of the day but slumping into my chair.

Unwilling to drop my number below 7,000, which I reserve for older people, like 87- or 88-year-olds, I began to divide my walks in half—3,500 steps twice a day. So far, that's working. But walks are not the same when I'm counting. They're an objective. I'm trying to upgrade my attitude and allow my gaze to rest upon the cactuses, none of which I can identify by name, although I have a book that will tell me—one I probably won't ever read. I try to locate a sense of goalless pleasure as I move up and down the calm streets of my new home.

My phone has a Health app. Entirely unbidden, a screen flashed, informing me that my walking asymmetry was 20.1, which was not a good number. I googled 'walking asymmetry' and entered my age, height, and weight, thinking that might be relevant, but I couldn't understand what walking asymmetry is, what mine should be, and who even asked my phone for its point of view. It appears I am walking on something of a slant, moving diagonally to get to where I want to go. I'm not slanted; my steps are—at least, according to my phone. I've decided to ignore it.

Twenty years ago, I bought a beautiful silver-handled walnut cane on impulse, thinking that someday, far in the future, when I might need such an object, I might as well have a gorgeous one. The cane was to be a rakish accessory, not a necessary accessory for balance, something I would wear with a Panama hat tilted just so. Currently, it's tucked away in my storage unit, waiting for its moment in the sun. This may be its moment. Perhaps my cane will help keep me on the straight and narrow as I walk. It's elegant, although the silver tip is an elaborately carved bird's head, and the beak sticks into my palm. A small price to pay, I've concluded, for a dramatic cane. Anyhow, nobody ever sees my palms. I'm thinking about using it. That's as far as I've gotten. It's hard to stride with a cane. Even diagonally.

I've had a couple of invitations to walk with women I've met here, but I continue to walk alone because I need to look where I'm going. My eldest daughter, a dancer, encourages me to stand up straight, with my face forward, and only my eyes looking down to avoid hunching over. I always smile and appreciate her suggestions, but I never follow them. I'm always peeking down to see if there is anything over which I would trip or fall. I'm my own alarm system and have to keep my eyes firmly on the ground to see where I'm going.

Once, after leaving a cafe with my daughter while walking back to our car, I turned to say something to her and missed a step on the sidewalk. Down I went. Nothing broke, although my left side ached and turned an ongoing series of unpleasant colors. That experience became an unavoidable warning that I needed to keep my eyes trained on the road ahead, not turned towards the face of the person I am with.

The result is that I also miss the clouds, the sky, the birds, the cactus, and the beauty all around me unless I stop to look around for a moment of pleasure, which I do. I can't talk and walk. I can't look around and walk. Those once benign behaviors have become dangerous. I take my steps while watching the ground for danger. I pause and look around. I take a drink, moving ever closer to successfully consuming the required ounces. I set out again. AARP would be proud of me.

As I unclasp my Apple Watch each night, I make sure the numbers register 7,000. I purposefully park a little further away from wherever I'm going and go down to get the mail the long way around. But that final thousand is getting harder, and I can sense that the time is fast approaching when I reprogram my Apple watch goal to six thousand, with five not too far behind. But, whatever the number, I'll keep stepping.

Three
Notes of an Intermittently Non-compliant Patient

Tucson is filled with retirees and snowbirds, but not enough doctors to go around. This requires me to try to find practitioners among the scant resources with my constellation of preexisting and current conditions that invariably accompany old age.

When I first arrived, my goal was to create a medical safety net for my body, every part of which now needs its own specialist. Eyes, ears, teeth, skin, lungs, heart, and kidneys require their own focused attention. I researched and chose practices focused on all the 'ologies' my body might need. Rheumatology, oncology, hematology, pulmonology, nephrology, dermatology. Plus, a dentist. A lesbian medical practitioner was always a plus in my determinations.

Preliminaries accomplished, I set about making my first appointments, which, as I had expected, were much further in the future than I'd imagined, and hoped that the relevant part of my body wouldn't need urgent medical attention before then. I created a spreadsheet to keep track of all my providers, starting with a geriatric primary care practice. That's me.

Geriatric. It was a promising beginning. My task was to stay healthy until I could be seen.

Nearly four months after I arrived in Tucson, I had a series of first appointments that involved achingly repetitive forms, family history, (much of which I made up because who even knows their grandparents' medical history—?)and was always conflicted during the weigh-in, when I could never decide whether to take off my sneakers and thus a few pounds, but left me needing to walk barefoot to the cubicle where I was to be seen. A young woman (always young and always woman) took my blood pressure, reviewed my medications—all without making eye contact—and rose, saying,

"The doctor will be with you shortly," the door firmly clicking shut behind her. After sitting in a closed room (I'm a little claustrophobic) for anywhere from ten to twenty minutes to await the doctor, there was a brief knock, the door swung open, and there he was. Yes—he.

Each of my specialists was different, but all of them were brisk—some even all the way to brusque. Upon entering the room, there was some patting, some pressing, and some paperwork for the specific type of blood work each specialty required, followed by a hurried, "Any questions?" before they were gone. But since these were all baseline exams without any active symptoms on my part, I didn't have any questions. Not yet anyhow. I simply began my relationship with these doctors feeling pissed off.

My rheumatologist wanted images to assess the spread of my rheumatoid arthritis. I didn't understand why those I already had from a year ago weren't sufficient. How much can

RA spread in a year when I wasn't having symptoms? In a temporarily compliant moment, I yielded to a dose of radiation, which at my advanced age probably doesn't make any difference anyway. It's like eating organic food. I eat organic fruits because they taste better, but not because I'll live even a second longer if I don't eat regular produce or drink regular milk. It's too late for all that.

With each of my successive visits, the doctor in question sweeps in, glances at my records, pulls up a rolling stool, stopping just short of my knees, and leans forward to ask about or palpate the specific organ that brought me there. That moment had usually been preceded by blood work, the results of which were posted on my patient portal and occasioned many hours of my googling what too high or too low means, resulting in my certainty that I had contracted several kinds of cancer. They typically handled all this stress-inducing information by saying,

"Your blood work looks good. No problems there."

That was the moment my compliance ended, beginning with my persistent questions about the "too-high" or "too-low" numbers.

"Can you recommend some articles I might read to help me better understand the variance in my blood work from last time?" I ask. His face clouds over. While he doesn't glance down at his watch, I feel as though he wants to. He recovers.

"Certainly. I'll have the nurse get them for you."

He doesn't say girl, but that's what I hear. This stiffens my spine. I charge on, "What about the interactions of the medications I'm taking for all my other issues? Are there any worries about contradictory responses?"

Now he sighs. I'm not going to make this easy for him. I'm not going to be a good patient. I'm going to sit there until he answers all my questions. However, there is sometimes the additional matter of clothing. Not having it on, I mean. That's a built-in vulnerability. It's hard to be authoritative on your own behalf without clothes.

I understand that the doctor's office should not have to be a place for consciousness-raising. These folks don't even know who I am, nor do they care. They deal with my heart, lungs, skin, eyes, and kidneys. I'm a carrier of those organs. Period. But I am unwilling to erase myself in the name of being a good patient. I am reluctant to yield to a doctor's old-fashioned idea, rigid ways of thinking, or hurriedly performing the most minimal engagement during my visits. After all, I'm from the generation of women who created Our Bodies, Our Selves.

When she was a girl, my mother learned that when going to the doctor, an occasion for which one wore their best clothes in preparation for the brief attention of a successful, professional Jewish man, one was careful not to ask too many questions, or, God forbid, for a second opinion. Any of those behaviors would hurt the doctor's feelings, and they wouldn't take good care of you anymore.

All her life, she continued to be concerned about her doctor's well-being, wanting them to like her, and she would often dress up for her appointments. Women of my mother's generation agreed with experts. They were the ones who told you what to do. That was their function. The first time an article, written by a doctor, appeared in the Boston Globe, suggesting that studies were beginning to indicate that smoking might be bad for you, my mother quit. That very day. After all, doctors knew more than the movie stars in the cigarette ads.

In her last years, when I accompanied her to medical appointments, she would shush me when I asked questions, while smiling apologetically at the doctor, as if I were an errant child. She sternly announced that she would allow me to take her (as if she could get there without me!), but I was not allowed to talk. I fully understood that lifelong patterns are lifelong for a reason, and I remained silent. Only later, after I returned her to the residential facility, did I research the issue that had been discussed, call the office, and ask my questions to either understand or challenge whatever it was the doctor had recommended. I assumed that the doctor's premise was that patients in their early nineties were considered disposable and therefore did not require careful attention. Comfort, pills for everything, and warm reassurance were the order of the day. Not for my mother. And not for me.

I am, at least for now, a maintenance patient, to be supervised every four or six months, monitoring my blood work and prescriptions, all that's required. Accordingly, I was transferred from the docs to the PAs in the practice, which was when my medical care improved. Drastically. Physician Assistants have the time, patience, curiosity, and interest, along with a wealth of valuable information. At least the ones I've been lucky enough to be handed off to, primarily because I wasn't medically interesting enough for the doctor himself.

Lucky me! Both to have women, yes, they are all women, interested in the me that surrounds the body part in question, raising issues I didn't even know enough to ask, and then providing unhurried and thorough answers. The care of my body now involves medications, supplements, sunscreen, and inhalers, all of which augment what was once my ability to begin the day by brushing my teeth.

My level of compliance also varies among the people I scarcely know who take it upon themselves to offer advice about my body. Sometimes the proffered suggestion isn't direct. It often follows a sigh or a long pause where the other person says, "Are you sure?" or a phrase designed to let me know I either don't have all the relevant facts or am simply being foolish. What often follows is, "I have a fabulous cranial-sacral person," or "Have you considered cutting out dairy?" All well-intentioned, to be sure, but options I might have already considered and dismissed. And cutting out dairy is entirely out of the question.

Internally, I bristle, even as externally, I smile and thank the speaker for their good ideas, while murmuring that it doesn't seem like a good fit for me. Of course, there's the standard generic advice that all of us oldies should follow. Eat wisely. Exercise as much as we can. Try not to drink or smoke if we can. Stuff like that. I do my best with those. But am I going to chant? I don't think so. Am I going to take chemo if I have a cancer that requires it? Nope. Not at 87. Do I want to hear extravagant praise about a yoga teacher or a rheumatologist? Not really. Perhaps a mild mention, prefaced by "if you're interested," might work, but probably not.

Then there are my daughters. My personality is not unfamiliar to them, and after all these decades (six!) of being my children, they know what to expect. To give them their middle-aged due, my girls often have good advice. And when they do, I take it. There is, however, a distinction between good advice and worried advice. I smile warmly through the latter.

My current relationship with compliance is variable, depending on my mood, the person or doctor offering the advice, my need to assert myself in our relationship, and the utility of the advice provided. But to be described as my mother was, as a compliant patient? Never. I will have both compliant and non-compliant responses and moments, and I'll be in charge of what those are and when they happen. And that's final.

Four
Tucson Book Festival Redux

By the end of my first year in Tucson, I was again chosen to have a three-hour slot at the Book Festival for *The Kitchen is Closed*. This time, I was confident and ready. I knew my way around. I'd done this before and was almost what you might call—a regular. At least I thought I was.

Selling books at open-air fairs requires shade. People walk faster in direct sunlight. Trust me. They move past the overly decorated booths, rarely stopping to browse. It's just too hot. Shade, on the other hand, is ideal for browsing. That is, if it's already more than a few hours into the fair. The serious bookies arrive early, do their purposeful shopping, then spend the remainder of the day strolling aimlessly up and down in front of the food booths, speaker booths, port-a-potty, and, of course, the overly eager booksellers who don't stand a chance with them.

This year, I was delighted to be assigned a book in the shade, but unlike last year, the sunny side of the street was filled with people strolling, browsing, and exclaiming. It was the shade that got the leftovers. Mothers with too many kids to manage, the overflow from a talk that was already full, and the lovers who only gazed into one another's eyes, not at the books they were passing.

I used the same easel board I had the year before on my assigned eight feet of picnic table, announcing:

Old. Jewish. Queer: All the Rest is Commentary.

I had a nicely fanned-out number of books, business cards, a bottle of water, five-dollar bills, and a pen. I even remembered to have a cloth to cover the table, one that I bought at a fabric store the day before. I was open for business.

As I settled into my assigned folding chair thirty minutes before things were to start, my picnic table mate arrived. She had written a romance novel about a southern belle (Southern belle? Do they even exist anymore?) She was elaborately made up, as were her daughters and, presumably, her heroine. Her eight feet of table quickly became covered with overlapping doilies, piles of her carefully arranged books, multiple scattered sachets, and a 4x6 stand-up plastic-covered statement identifying her Venmo and Facebook accounts. Plastic sprays representing boughs of apples, at least I think they were meant to be apples, lent the concluding flourish. After she had completed her preparations, she and her two daughters posed for selfies. Lots of women authors around me were taking selfies. Author-ish ones, smiling ones, concluding with a series where everyone sticks out their tongues or makes a moue with their lips. Why is that a thing?

I've noticed that there is a predictable tempo when straight people pass my easel. They walk faster, fearing perhaps the easel will reach out and grab them, not releasing their hold until they convert them to homosexuality. Then there are the queer men who circle my booth a couple of times before approaching me because I apparently don't look like most people's idea of a queer. I look like a tall old woman with a pleasant face. After a few passes, they'd approach and begin,

"Did you write this book?"

"I did," I respond, with my ever-widening, determinedly approachable smile, after which a conversation ensues, many interesting, some touching. Gay men often begin with their homosexual history before asking me how long I've been a lesbian and when I became one. Then we discuss our shared points of reference. Gradually, I steer the companionable anecdotes to the book I'm selling. It's the old part that seems to unsettle people. It seems people are comfortable calling themselves queer these days, but balk at using the word old. Even when they most decidedly are. I can tell.

Then there are old dykes who flip through the pages, get what the book is right away, and announce, "I'll get a copy for myself, and sometimes they add firmly, "and a couple more for friends who need to read this." After their decision is made, we fall into an old lesbian conversation. Young lesbians and young queer people want to buy the book for some old person in their life and tell me stories about them as they're fishing in their wallets for money. No young person appears to carry cash anymore. My daughters tried to convince me to use Venmo or Square, but I haven't. It's just another thing to learn.

That's the old and the queer crowd. The Jewish heterosexual customers get a bit stymied by queer but duck the subject and talk about where they grew up. It's one of the ways Jews identify themselves to one another.

"You're a Jew? I grew up in Flushing."

Then I nod, and we are, briefly, two Jews together.

Three people stopped thinking I had written a cookbook, and one man carrying a newly purchased copy of American Serial Killers paused and looked at me for an uncomfortably long time before moving on. Several heterosexual couples saw the title, after which the wife playfully notified her husband,

"That's what I want, too. A closed kitchen," she said with a conspiratorial wink, as though I might somehow be pressed into service to facilitate her domestic life.

There was an ongoing repetition as I rose and sat down, ascended and descended, up and down, in and out of the folding chair each presenter was allotted. That was the old part. I wanted to stand alongside or behind my display, looking inviting, but after fifteen or twenty minutes, I'd need to sit down again. If I saw someone approaching who looked like a potential purchaser, I leapt to my feet, just in case. So, I sprang forward and fell back, like daylight savings time, which did not result in respite for my legs, and then, as time went on, my hips, back, shoulders, and neck.

Finally, my shift was over; the next batch of eager authors arrived, standing impatiently watching us packing our literary offerings, leaving the picnic table pristine for their moment in the sun—or, in this case, shade. Rolling my suitcase, happily lighter than when I arrived, I passed the booths of hundreds of authors, community and religious organizations, musicians, and food trucks, and made my proud, exhausted, and satisfied way home.

By the end of my second year in Tucson, I had completed the book about my nine months in Phoenix called *Leaving Home at 83*. It was published by Rattling Good Yarns, a mission-driven LGBTQI+ press, and chosen to be represented at the Tucson Festival of Books. This was to be my third outing! I ordered a large easel board featuring the book's cover, business cards with the cover image on one side and my contact information on the other, and a colorful cloth to adorn the utilitarian folding table that would be supplied. I was becoming an old hand at this!

Alas, my third opportunity to shine was not to be. COVID interrupted my best-laid plans and required me to substitute my elegant tunic and red earrings for faded pajamas with—inexplicably—menorahs all over them that Ally had gifted me the previous Chanukkah. Maybe next year. Maybe even for the book you're holding in your hands or reading on your screen right now.

Part Two
Living While Old

Five
Hearing and Seeing—At the Same Time

While I am no longer six feet tall, an elevation alarmingly reached at the end of my thirteenth summer, I'm still a reasonably upright five feet nine and a half inches. I'm no longer haunted by being called a long drink of water or being taunted, "How's the air up there?," hoping for boyfriends even taller than me to dance and kiss with, deciding whether to wear flats (big feet make flats look like canoes even if they're dyed to match your dress), or little kitten heels which make me cuter in the leg department but even taller than everyone else. Those youthful vulnerabilities are thankfully a distant memory. Now that I'm very old, being tall is no longer a source of shame, having become the eventual pride it has been all these years. Instead, the issue is that the combination of my height and hearing impairment leaves me having to choose between seeing and hearing.

As my audible range diminished, I gradually learned the tricks of someone who is hard of hearing. First, and most critically, it became essential that I directly face the person I was talking with. We had to be in immediate proximity because if they were moving around their apartment while talking to me, I'd only be able to hear every fifth word and lose the thread of what was being said by the end of the first paragraph. The alternative might be to get up and follow the speaker around, but that's not always possible, or even seemly.

I can no longer walk with several of my closest friends (those who still walk) because they are too short. When we attempt a conversation, their words emerge into the air somewhere around bosom level, not nearly close enough to my ears to be received. My desire to make warm, engaged eye contact with them is undermined by my need to follow their lips as they speak. I look down from my height and try to shift my eyes upwards from lips to eyes periodically, so the speaker knows I'm in good emotional connection with them, but return as quickly as I can to their mouths in case I miss something they are currently saying.

My intense focus on their mouths while remaining connected with their eyes has to be balanced with coding obstacles in the path and uneven curbs. Looking down at the ground, up at the face, down to the lips, up to the eyes, it's a bit of choreography that, as you can imagine, makes taking walks with friends much less pleasurable than it once was. And that's not all. I now have the additional constraint of diminished breathing capacity after surgery for lung cancer removed a lobe of my lung, so walking and talking at the same time causes breathlessness. These days, navigating all that is involved with walking, talking, hearing, and not falling is no longer an option.

As a result, my friends and I travel in silence, randomly smiling cheerfully at one another. Our conversations don't begin until we arrive at a café and are seated. Even then, there is the additional issue of my squirming. Because of my aforementioned tallness and the preponderance of regular-sized people chairs, I've always found it challenging to get comfortably situated in a position that fits my legs, which is newly compounded by the unsettling fact that my thirteen-year-old knee replacement appears to be loosening its grip and is sliding around. It's something about my ligaments. I've never been entirely sure what a ligament is, except that it's good to stretch but not pull them. So, I'm left, constantly rearranging my aching super-long legs in chairs that don't allow me to achieve either comfort or stillness. I worry that when I've been squirming for too long, I appear either restless or disinterested in what my companion is saying, so I re-fasten my gaze firmly upon her to reconnect us, thus missing what's recently come out of her mouth. It's a lose-lose situation.

Don't even get me started about ambient noise. There's no getting around it. It's everywhere. It's always been everywhere, except it once used to be called music, a nearby conversation, ordinary street traffic, a plane flying overhead, or simply the hum of life. Now it's noise. Noise that prevents me from hearing what is being said, and for which I need to respond. After all, there are only so many times a person can say WHAT? Or my attempt at a more charming HMMM? I need silence to hear. And the world is never silent.

I was in my early forties when more friends than I could ignore told me that I was losing my hearing. After huffily discounting all their concerns, often accompanied by a sigh and an eye roll on my part, I succumbed and went for a hearing test. Hearing aids, it was. Forty years ago, hearing aids were big, uncomfortable, cumbersome, and obvious. I changed my hairstyle to cover my ears, hoping to conceal the large, orange, peanut-shaped objects stuffed into them. In the intervening decades, I've lived through multiple iterations of their evolution. My current pair is invisible, computer-programmed, and allows me to switch between settings for restaurants, music, outdoors, and everyday usage. I never remember to change the settings, though, so they remain at normal, which, so far, works. Even with my state-of-the-art hearing aids, there remains the necessity for a quiet room in which to hear. Places with more than four people animatedly conversing require me to get closer to the speaker than might be comfortable for them.

Things are not necessarily more manageable in the quiet environment of plays and movies, even with my hearing aids set on high. When the main character turns away in disgust, anger or fear, and says what turns out to be the pivotal phrase of the scene, all I can see is the side of their face or the back of their head and am unable to hear a single word. Or when our heroine breaks down, covering her face with her hand as she sobs, and then behind all that noisy crying and hidden face-- speaks. And murmuring lovers in the movies? Forget it. That is a signal failure of moviemaking, if you ask me, and it causes me to lose the central plot pivot, leaving me unclear about why the rest of the film unfolds as it does.

Subtitled foreign films are one of my great pleasures since I'm an expert at flicking my eyes up and down from mouth to text at great speed. Closed captioning is a relief from sitting just inches from the television screen or worrying that I'm annoying the neighbors by having the volume at what seems like a good level for me. I don't have to make eye contact with the people on the screen, and I can briefly look away to reach for my popcorn while still hearing just fine.

I imagine a future where inventors figure out how to give everyone their own built-in closed captioning, a cartoon bubble that displays their words, so that tall, hard-of-hearing old women with breathing issues and bad knees can maintain eye contact and know what is being said—even if the speaker is crying or turned away. Are there any AI entrepreneurs out there reading this? The future is waiting for you—at least I am.

Six
Confessions of a Lying Mother

I live alone, and living alone requires a certain degree of lying. There's no way around it. It isn't that I mean to lie; it's that I want to avoid the conversation that will immediately ensue if I don't. The people who monitor my life, as in my daughters, need to feel reassured that I'm eating healthily, exercising regularly, getting enough sleep, and staying engaged. Engaging means different things to them than to my aging friends; but they are the ones to whom I must answer.

I call what I do many things. Leaving things out. Looking at the positive side. But my kids are nobody's fool and don't miss very much; if one does, the other straightens her out. They're in cahoots about their mother, and I have practically no hiding places left. I'm becoming nearly as much of an open book to my kids as I am to my women friends, and I'm left to reconsider where my sense of privacy is these days.

I assure them I eat vast quantities of fruits, vegetables, salmon, and chicken. There is rarely any mention of my consumption of popcorn, rum-raisin ice cream, or pistachio nuts. When we're having a meal together, I'm careful to order a big slab of protein surrounded by leafy green vegetables. I demur when offered crackers and cheese and murmur daintily with a downcast expression.... dairy. Until they read this, I'll continue to feel confident I've gotten away with those lies.

There are days I don't want to eat my meals in the prescribed order. What if I want something other than cereal, eggs, or toast for breakfast, like the leftover takeout from the Chinese restaurant? Well, then, that's what I do. Sometimes, my disorderly eating leads to the need for Alka-Seltzer, but I keep a supply on hand for such occasions. Do I think my daughters check my medicine cabinet? I'm not sure. Probably not, but just in case, I keep the Alka-Seltzer tucked away out of sight. I want to avoid answering the questions about why I need it.

I lie—not only by indirection but also by omission-- about the frequency of my accidents. They include tripping over, stumbling into, brushing against, and, worst of all, falling all the way down. I try not to bump into anything, but I fail. Repeatedly. Even when I rush to the freezer to urgently press an ice cube onto the spot, an enormous purple bruise blossoms under it.

But it's not just that I bang into things, causing bruises or skin tears, resulting in bleeding. Old women have paper-thin skin, and every little thing ends up with an eruption of blood, requiring covering, which results in my arms being festooned with bandages. I have to try to get them on with one hand while holding a cloth over the bleeding with the other, resulting in a wastepaper basket filled with false starts and discarded adhesive. My medicine chest currently has a larger supply of bandages of every size and shape, multiple forms of gauze and tape, and tubes of healing ointments than I ever needed when my children were little.

When I go out all bandaged up, I'm met with concerned gazes and the question, "Are you okay?" I smile nonchalantly and say, "You should see the other guy." Their smiling response allows me to circumvent whatever concrete lie I would have to create to explain my multi-colored, multi-textured arms.

Sleeves were initially advertised for gardeners, which makes sense, like those knee pads for doing whatever gardeners do on their knees. Now, a wide range of sleeves with various designs are used as arm accessories. Some with tattoos might be fun. I can lie and pretend I'm making a fashion statement while covering my ongoing cascade of wounds.

Then there are the moments when the urgent task of keeping my balance eludes me entirely, and I fall all the way down. This is most often the result of my trying to multitask. Not balancing two thoughts at a time, which has become entirely out of the question. One of the two disappears into the ether almost at once. I now fail at navigating two physical tasks at the same time. My most recent fall occurred in the parking lot of my apartment building. I was getting out of the car, wheeling my grocery cart with one hand and reaching back to close the car door with the other—a recipe for disaster. Down I went onto the concrete, the cart rolling to a stop three feet ahead of me against the bumper of a nearby parked car. My first impulse was to look around. Not for help, which would have been the adult thing to do. But to see if anyone saw me go down. I was alone, which allowed me to turn over onto my hands and knees—which is how I get up from the ground these days.

I'm uncertain if not letting my daughters know I fell constitutes withholding necessary information, yet another permutation of lying, but I suspect it does. Why is it anyone's business? They'll just worry and offer advice, which are bromides I already know. Be careful. Only do one thing at a time. Move slowly. Use Arnica. The only person who knew I fell is my Apple Watch, which dutifully flashed me a question. I see you fell. Do you need help? Should I call 911? I pressed back; I'm fine, I lied, in whatever language they have programmed for a response. I hobbled upstairs, hurriedly put the freezer food in the freezer and the refrigerator food in the refrigerator, then lay down and went to sleep. I've concluded that I am handling the situation maturely.

There are more things that I lie about to my daughters. Well, not exactly lying. I just never mention them. Like losing, followed by forgetting. I'm a very tidy woman. Everything in my home has a designated spot where it resides, a clear and obvious one, so that it's easy to find when I need to retrieve it. Order comforts me. But even in my carefully put-together home, I lose things. While they turn up in a pants pocket, lost at the bottom of my bag, or stuck between a pile of papers on my desk, I never understand how that came to be their momentary resting place. I lose things outside my house as well. In public bathrooms, I sometimes take the opportunity to check my messages, then carefully balance the phone on the toilet paper dispenser-- and leave it there. I'm up to three times on that one, and each time, it required the kindness of strangers. I'm hoping my luck holds out. At the sad conclusion of my early marriage, I lost my house keys twice in one week. Sometimes, there is meaning in losing. Not anymore. There are no metaphors to explore here.

Talking out loud is a new and comforting development in my living alone. It isn't that I want another person's voice in my apartment; I just want a voice. And mine does just fine. "I think I'll watch Hacks," I say brightly. Then I get up from my desk, walk into the living room, and do just that. It's a little like having non-demanding company. I enjoy talking to myself and continue to find myself sprightly.

I lose words—of course I do. I'm old. I even lose entire trains of thought. But I remember enough to keep myself interested and do my best to decide that whatever I forgot wasn't essential or that the thought would return. But when it does, it's often in the midst of something else where it doesn't fit, and I don't understand why I'm remembering whatever it is. Sometimes, when I lose words, I find others to substitute. Recently, when reaching for the phrase Secret Service, I said instead, Social Security. My daughter looked puzzled by my introducing this unexpected phrase into our conversation, and I hurriedly substituted what I meant to say. Secret Service. This kind of thing is happening more and more often. You can't pretend about some things—especially those you said right out loud. Then I have to navigate my embarrassment with a lie, followed by my annoyance at my embarrassment. My kids detect every instance of my forgetting and, even worse, the moments when I go entirely blank. That's pretty recent.

Behind my agreeable face is an old woman holding fiercely to her wavering autonomy. I wonder if middle-aged children of aging parents yield to parental obfuscations and equivocations because they may not want to know about the realities that define their parents' lives, like forgetting, falling, creative eating, losing, bumping into sharp objects, and talking to themselves. Does their worried concern mask a protectiveness against the reality that the more they know, the more they may have to step towards us and our increasingly precarious hold on independence and fold us into their lives. Because that's where all this is going, isn't it? Our lying is buying us the time we want as our own. And I'll continue to lie as long as I can get away with it.

But that time will come. And then I will have to face my greatest fear about aging. Being a burden on my daughters' lives. I know we all may eventually become a responsibility for our children, those of us who have children. At least, children with whom we're on good terms, which can narrow down the playing field. In the best case, we'll become a welcome disruption in their lives and choices, albeit a disruption, nonetheless. There's just no way around it. For those of us without children, we may have chosen to focus on family, friends, community members, and neighbors. But they may also be old. While my friends understand more about life, themselves, and me, they can't help me in concrete ways. None of us can get down on the floor to retrieve something that has rolled under the sofa or climb the stepladder to reach the canister on the top shelf. There is help, like a casserole when I'm sick,-- and then there is jeopardizing my friend's well-being.

Belonging to a synagogue, church, or community organization with a wellness committees, and having neighbors in their healthy fifties, all provide options for aging folks. But for many of us, it's our kids. Somehow.

I'm down at the bedrock of things now, a time I have been able to hold at bay. After a lifetime of writing, teaching, organizing, activism, travel, and friendships—a life I carved out of the rocky soil of my early years—I've had most of the life I dreamed for myself. Over the past decade, my daughters have stepped forward to care for me as the inevitability of replacing my joints with titanium, removing a thyroid after a cancer diagnosis, and then another surgery, to remove a part of my lung. They were loving and present, and I sank gratefully into their care. But somehow, for me, at least, all of that was situational. I'd get better, which I did, and they'd leave to return to their lives, which they did. But I'm approaching a time when I won't get better, when they won't be able to return to their lives because I'll have to become an ongoing part of those lives. It won't be me wanting them anymore. It will be me needing them, dependent on their nearness, attending to the details of my life; I will no longer be able to manage on my own.

So much of my lying to my daughters has been predicated on my need to maintain my independence, to be on my own, answering only to myself. I love that about my life. And while I know my daughters will welcome my presence lovingly, I don't want to be welcomed. I want to live on my own and die in my bed with no Depends or Ensure or bottles of pills on the bedside table, along with all the other accoutrements of the end of life that have marked the deaths of my beloveds. Just me in the bed, looking up at whoever is there, saying a couple of tender goodbyes, closing my eyes, and dying. Just like in the movies. Except in the movies, they always wear eye makeup while dying. I'll skip that part. Although I suppose I will have bedhead, but I can live—and die with that.

I remember my phone calls with my mother when I was in my 60s, and she was my age. It was important for her to know what I was doing in my hectic and active life, and I always provided the highlights. But the more granular details—the love affair limping towards its end, the fear that my job might be unstable, the menopausal mood swings. Those remained unsaid. I wanted and needed her to feel everything was alright with me. That I was okay. That she didn't need to worry about me. Then, I'd ask,

"And you, Ma? Are you okay?" She'd always respond,

"Yes, honey. Everything here is good."

I understand now; she needed me to think everything was all right. She never spoke about her loneliness, the hours she spent looking out of her front window, watching cars pull up to the entrance of her apartment building, releasing families who had come to spend the day. Grandchildren who arrived to see their grandmothers. She never asked if she could come for a visit, worried that there would be a pause, just a beat too long, when I might tell her that it wasn't a good time---perhaps in the summer when the children were out of school, and my work slowed up. And I never thought to ask what she felt when looking out of the window.

I saw my mother through 60-year-old eyes, the same eyes through which my daughters see me. My mother was a proud woman, as am I. But as reading became difficult, as speech became an awkward excursion through a field of scattered and lost words that fled as she approached, as walking required appliances to maintain her balance -- objects she would never use in public, as her hearing diminished and she was unwilling to get hearing aids because they would show, even under her well-coiffed hair -- her life grew smaller and more isolated, quieter and sadder.

She kept much of her life from me, imagining she was behaving appropriately, not being a complaining mother, putting forward a good face to her children, values she took seriously, and not wanting to burden or upset me. She didn't want to reveal any diminishment of her carefully curated autonomy. Her fear of becoming a needy old woman led her to reveal only partial truths and contradictory stories. Our long-distance phone calls were filled with her attempts to reassure me that all was well, even as I sensed that so much remained unspoken, both of us ending the call unsatisfied.

I flew across the country to visit her and assess, as my daughters do with me now, how well she was doing. Of course, she knew that was my agenda, so she was on her best behavior to reassure me that she was still fine. When I suggested installing grab rails in the bathtub, she assured me she didn't need them, concluding,

"You can come in with me. I'll show you."

My mother had accompanied me into the bathroom when I was a child, bathing me, braiding my hair, and checking to be sure I'd brushed my teeth. Now, the tables were turning, and I wasn't sure how I felt about that. But I sat on the toilet seat as the bathtub filled, and she undressed. Swinging her frail leg over the bathtub's edge as she held tightly to the faucet with both hands, she sank to one knee, then slowly brought her other leg across the enameled edge and shifted from kneeling to lowering herself to sit in the water. Looking up at me with pride, she said,

"See? I told you I could get in the tub by myself. You don't need to worry about me. I'm fine managing by myself. I don't need some stranger looking at me naked. It's none of their business."

I searched for the words that would allow my mother to maintain her dignity and hear my concerns.

"But Ma. It's slippery. Maybe I can put some strips on the bottom of the tub."

"I don't want strips. What for? I'm holding on. It's fine, honey. Stop worrying."

She soaped up her washcloth, gliding it over her thin, mottled skin as I made an excuse to leave the bathroom for a minute, pretending I needed something so she would wash what she called her 'privates' privately.

When I re-entered the steamy bathroom, she showed me her exit strategy, which involved letting all the water drain out of the tub, returning to her hands and knees, swinging first one leg, then the other, over the side of the tub, and holding onto the sink to straighten up. She stood before me naked, glistening with drops of water, triumphant.

"I told you there's nothing to be fussing about." I smiled up at her, swallowing my words of concern.

I dutifully called every Sunday morning to check in, concerned that her driving had become more circumscribed after she described going to the market the first thing in the morning because the parking lot was still full of what she described as easy spaces. I heard what that meant, but allowed myself to be comforted by the fact that she was wise enough to shop at a time of day that was comfortable for her. I accepted her reassurances because I would've had to do something if I hadn't.

When she told me she loved buying big, sweet potatoes because she put them in the microwave, and they made a wonderful dinner, I didn't say,

"Ma, that's not dinner. That's a potato." I pretended instead that she was doing what she could manage in the kitchen. I told myself I was proud of her creativity, and she promised always to be careful.

She wasn't exactly lying, leaving things out (although she might have been), or even putting on a good face. My mother was holding onto her diminishing autonomy and did not want to be a burden on my life. I understand her now and can imagine exactly how she must have felt. But then, like I imagine my daughters are with me now, I was worried and frustrated.

On a recent visit, Janaea wheeled my laundry cart filled with groceries into the kitchen and announced in a firm voice,

"See, Ma? You're not supposed to lift, and it would be better to have your groceries delivered."

"Here's where you're wrong," I responded firmly. "Completely and utterly wrong. Watch this!"

Going into my office, I sat down in my desk chair and wheeled myself down the hall and into the kitchen, where I rolled to a stop beside the cart, positioned it between me and the refrigerator, and began to unpack the groceries from a comfortable seated position, only occasionally glancing up to see the grudging expression of approval on my daughter's face.

"I can handle the groceries just fine, honey. I told you there's nothing to worry about." She swallowed her words just as I had. Now, sometimes, like my mother, I will microwave a big potato, slather it with butter and scallions, and call it dinner.

My daughters watch me as I adapt, defend, and protect, exchanging glances when I forget a word or misplace the TV remote. Checking that I put my seatbelt on as soon as I get in the car, Janaea recently asked if I thought my driving wasn't just "a little too zippy."

They have outgrown their need for me to know the details of their lives, and I don't want to burden them with the details of mine. I'm careful not to complain during our phone calls, and I put a positive spin on my life. I don't say I worry about my memory, my finances, or my arthritis. But I don't want them to end our phone calls feeling unsatisfied because I have been unable to tell them what they need and want to know. We navigate my need for autonomy and desire to make my own decisions with their need for my safety, comfort, and well-being.

I continue to try to come forward with my daughters while holding onto myself, and I can see my mother's life so much more clearly now that she is dead, and I am old. To allow my mind and my heart to wander through all the doorways, she kept closed to protect herself and me. I want to go back twenty-five years and put my arms around her to tell her I understand why she stubbornly held on to her competencies, even as they were eroding and disappearing. I want her to know I was happy to fold her into my life (mostly), and I know her granddaughters feel the same way about me (mostly); that's as good as this time of life gets. Children who love me, watch and worry about me, and are proud of my self-reliance, even as they know it's increasingly temporary. That's what I have. And that's what she had. We would sit on her beloved itchy crewelwork sofa, feeling the loss and the pride of this moment. Together.

Seven
My Last Waltz

I was ready, suitcase bulging with all the accessories an old tourist might need. Nan, my oldest friend and a woman with whom I had traveled many times before, and I were going to New Orleans for the Jazz Festival as part of a Road Scholar trip. We'd learn from experts and have all the small details of moving around taken care of. That was the plan, anyhow.

I had prepared for every potential eventuality. The cuisine was rich and spicy, so since I was not planning to exercise a single drop of self-restraint on this trip, an abundance of Alka-Seltzer went into my toiletries bag. All my medications were carefully parceled out by day, time of day, and extras, just in case. There were replacement parts for my hearing aids, bandages in multiple sizes for wounds ranging from minor to severe, Voltaren for generalized arthritic aches, batteries and cords for every contingency, and, of course, sunscreen. I was ready.

But, as it became evident nearly at once, I wasn't. I've attended music festivals and concerts in open-air venues and large arenas all my life. They're always crowded, but never too crowded to keep the audience from dancing and the attendees from milling around. I've danced. I've milled. I've sung along, fueled by the energy of everyone around me. These days, I need a lot of that energy to even get to the event in question. There are traffic-filled streets, long lines at security, and then sitting squished into a small seat on a cross-country plane ride to even arrive amongst the swaying, singing, arm-waving multitude. Balance has become another central consideration. Keeping it, I mean. Once, my delight in being present at a massive festival and moving through a sea of revelers didn't carry any unease about the possibility of stumbling, tripping, or bumping into. Remaining upright wasn't in my mind; flinging myself into the midst of things was.

After all the stress of flying across the country, with salted crackers as the primary food group and a layover in our hub city requiring intra-airport trains to get from one gate to the other, we gratefully arrived at our hotel, unpacked, and fell into an exhausted sleep. The next morning, before anything was to begin, I began.

I felt the fall happening in slow motion. Once the skid began, as I turned from the sink towards the shower, my foot refused to follow my brain's urgent command to stop it at once! and instead continued on its inevitable trajectory. I fell and smashed my face against the edge of the bathtub, splitting my lip and causing an extravagant geyser of blood all over me, the floor, and the towels I reached for and was anxiously patting myself with. I reached into my mouth to wiggle my teeth to make sure they were still firmly housed and hadn't been shaken loose. After rising and facing the mirror, I saw what my face looked like underneath all that blood. My lips were cut and vastly puffed up like liposuction gone terribly wrong.

Nan, uncharacteristically, was unable to locate any comforting words when I said,

"How terrible do I look?"

She stood in the doorway of the bathroom looking both protective and stricken, and murmured,

"Oh my," then paused, reaching for a reassuring smile, "it will fade in a few days."

I took that to mean really terrible.

I entered the first breakfast of the Road Scholars in the ballroom of the Hotel Monteleone, determined not to avert my face apologetically when speaking but careful not to make eye contact. I said, as per our instructions, my name, why I came, and what I was looking forward to. At that moment, I was looking forward to some ice and my return to a soft bed.

After everyone had spoken, our trip guide provided an introduction to all the splendors that awaited us. The dozens of performance stages that are scattered around the French Quarter and along the Mississippi River. The events featuring Cajun, Creole, Zydeco, blues, brass bands, piano players, singers, dance lessons, and, for sustenance, food trucks with every cuisine of the region. This was the largest free festival in the country, she said with great enthusiasm; then paused, her voice deepening to signal seriousness, and added a caveat, smiling gamely throughout: "There are the streets. The French Quarter has potholes, uneven sidewalks, and other dangers, so it's important to look down as you walk to avoid falling." Looking down defeats the purpose of moving through a festival, but I'd happily comply. Falling down was something I had already done just a few hours before, and once was enough.

The inauspicious morning was salvaged, however, by the first of our series of morning concerts and lectures, which illuminated the richness and history of New Orleans music. The fact that everyone was facing front while the musicians talked and played relievedly allowed me to temporarily overlook my face, and now, the growing pain in both my knee and my arm. It was only upon rising and trying to move around that I realized a trip to Walgreens was in order. A sling, Tylenol, and some concealer were the best I could do. The wind wasn't entirely out of my sails, although they were most decidedly drooping, so I persevered. I hadn't come all this way to be vain and foolish—even though it was too late. I already was.

That afternoon, Nan and I made our way over to one of the stages closest to the hotel while dutifully looking down at the street. At least I did. Nan strode, which made my mincing feel like forlorn walking. Since it was the first day of the festival and not yet the weekend, the crowds hadn't swelled to what eventually became tens of thousands of exuberant fans.

The group of women, backed by a brass band, singing old Delta blues, was rowdy and unrestrained. I attempted to emulate their boisterousness by dancing with my left leg and right arm, throwing what remained of my caution to the wind, and was reminded why I wanted to come to the festival. That is, until a combination of sun and pain set in, mostly in my arm and knee, and we headed back.

The Road Scholar folks had given each of the participants a folding chair to carry to the festival, which, were I still merely 80 years old, might have been lightweight, but with my only partially functioning body, felt cumbersome and awkward. Nevertheless, the next day, after another glorious morning concert/lecture, off I marched, this time on my own. Nan needed a quiet day, so I slung the chair over my good shoulder, eyes focused on potential potholes and uneven cobblestones, and I joined an increasingly large, raucous, and fast-moving crowd. It was hot, and while I had a rakish straw hat, or at least I hoped it looked rakish, sunscreen on my exposed arms, and sturdy sneakers on my feet, my tempo appeared to keep getting in the way of everyone trying to move forward. I was a human boulder in the sea of ebbing and flowing, enthusiastic, and young festival goers.

I made it all the way to the Mississippi River, which was probably no more than a mile or two away, but felt like I had been walking for days. There were several stages, each featuring a different form of New Orleans music, along with purveyors of everything from beads to palm readings, food trucks with long lines, and riverboats with their own bands moving up and down the river. It was a visual advertisement, a worthy image of a glorious music festival. The sun glistened on the water, the boats moved majestically up and back, filled with dancing revelers, and the grass was covered with folks seated on chairs like the one I carried, although the most seasoned among them had umbrellas as well. There was a rich array of musical choices, but no benches upon which to sit, and not one single drop of shade.

Given the paucity of options, I approached a stage where a piano player/singer was maintaining a deep groove. I opened the chair I had been lugging around, and sank into it, planning to ignore the sun and enjoy the music. But as I sank, I realized that the chair was lower to the ground than I had anticipated, which would make getting up a multi-pronged process. In public. These days, if I have to get up from the floor, I turn over onto all fours and push myself up, which works perfectly, but those moves were never anything I intended to do outside the privacy of my own home. I gave myself a stern talk, telling myself to quiet down, sit here, and enjoy the music, the energy, the New Orleans-ness of it all. My ability to follow my own instructions lasted about fifteen minutes, after which I began plotting moderately sinuous ways of rising so I could head back to the cool respite of the hotel. After much pushing down and falling back, I made it to my feet (and, of course, nobody but me was paying attention to me) and began the trek back.

The trudge back to the hotel felt like it took twice as long as it did to get to the venue. I made it to the room, fell across the bed, and slept, awakening just in time for our first group dinner, which would require both my presence and the capacity for speech. I had already gathered from the questions asked of the musicians at our morning lecture that many of the folks on this trip were knowledgeable, so I hoped that would offer me a sufficient entry point into dinner table conversation. Also, I was hungry, and while I already had as much stimulation as I could manage for the day and longed for silence, hunger won out. Nan and I went off to meet our co-Road Scholars.

The tour guides had selected the best restaurants in the city for each of our dinners, and I was looking forward to enjoying the local cuisine and engaging in animated discussions about music. But to my chagrin, the people on either side and just across from me (the only ones I could hear) wanted to let others know where they were from and the pros and cons of their earlier trips. I tried to steer the conversation around to New Orleans music with little success, although if the room hadn't been crowded and noisy, I could have been more specific in my questions. But given that I was yelling, and they were whispering (at least that's how it seemed), I yielded to the subject matters du jour, ate everything put in front of me, all of which was as mouth-watering as advertised, and waited for the very first opportunity to return to my bed.

After another brilliant morning lecture and demonstration, the afternoon schedule included the welcome relief of a bus tour. Sitting down all day was just my speed. Our guide was a man steeped in local traditions, knowledgeable about the history and life of the various neighborhoods, who offered vivid and heartbreaking descriptions of Katrina and its aftermath, the history of regional architectural forms, and the iconography of the city's many cemeteries. We disembarked at all the places of significance, with our last stop at the New Orleans Art Museum, adjacent to the Sculpture Garden. We were briefly free to be on our own. I was grateful not to have to look down at the street while navigating the crowds—I could walk on a paved, level path, which I celebrated with two beignets in an adjoining café.

The downside of our splendid tour was that the air conditioning in the bus had gone on its own holiday, and we were sitting in stale, moist heat throughout the day. But everyone was trying to be cheerful—they had paid a lot for this adventure after all—and I prided myself on being a good sport and, except for exchanging glances with Nan, didn't complain. That's one of the many advantages of traveling with a woman who has been an intimate friend for 35 years. A glance is all it takes to communicate everything that needs to be said.

The next morning, after the concert and lecture, which focused on the role of the brass band and the history of second lines, we decided to forgo the task of navigating the crowds in the French Quarter, along with whatever musical treats we were sure to miss. We returned to the Sculpture Garden and the Museum to immerse ourselves in a day of age-appropriate calm, appreciating the wide-ranging collections of art, culture, politics, and beauty that this port city had to offer.

In the Lyft heading back to our hotel, Nan said she hoped we'd be on time to meet up with our group in the hotel lobby before they left for the restaurant. My spirits sank. She assumed we were going to end our day with dinner in another noisy, crowded, busy restaurant, but I didn't want to break the spell of our serene day.

One of the significant differences between us is that Nan is, and has always been, a responsible participant. I mean to be, and sometimes I succeed, but fundamentally, I'm not. Getting out of things I don't want to do doesn't present a problem for me, except for figuring out how to do it without causing too much discomfort or hurting anyone's feelings. For Nan, signing up for Road Scholars meant she was committed to being part of their programming and would attend all their scheduled events. I am more equivocal about the showing-up thing.

She gracefully yielded to my need for a quiet dinner on our own, during which we both acknowledged our eagerness to get home and decided to skip the last breakfast and move our plane reservations to an earlier hour. We found the group leader, offered our appreciation for her skillful leadership, and said our goodbyes. The following morning, instead of joining the departing throng in yet another restaurant, Nan and I retraced our steps through long security lines, salted crackers (the salad bar wasn't open yet, and there wasn't a single banana in the entire Denver concourse. I know. I walked its whole length in my fruitless search).

As she and I said our goodbyes, I returning to Tucson, and she to Berkeley; Nan gently suggested (all of Nan's suggestions are gentle, which is one of the many reasons our friendship has been so wonderfully gratifying) that I consider getting a wheelchair at the airport so I wouldn't have to stand in long lines, and could enjoy the comfort of being whisked around a busy airport. I assured her I might do just that, but as I entered the concourse, I saw it wasn't very crowded (it was late morning on a Thursday) and decided that I'd get a wheelchair next time. However, as of this moment, I knew I could manage my rolling suitcase without any help, which I did. It's my pride. An upright and sturdy old woman making her way across the concourse with her wheelie bag, her overstuffed carry-on, and her jacket, all powered by her tightly laced sneakers, is how I want to see myself. Running through my mind is, *I can do this. I can still do this. I still want to be able to do this. Maybe I can't do this. There will come a time when I won't be able to do this.* A wheelchair is what comes next.

After boarding, an enormous muscular man in a tracksuit, thus emphasizing his musculature, tapped my shoulder as I sat vacantly in the aisle seat, mind emptied of everything but wanting to get home. He clearly wanted to move towards the window and did so, settling into his seat with an enormous man spread. Rather than irritatingly averting my eyes from this display of entitlement to space, I saw in his posture a positive outcome. If I emulated him, we might be able to protect the middle seat and have more space for our/my legs. I mimicked his stance, and while it felt awkward and unfamiliar, I did manage, along with pretending to be asleep, to keep the middle seat clear for the flight.

After we took off, he removed a vibrator from his red leather backpack and began lovingly rubbing it over his chest and arms, inserting it into his armpit (I don't know what muscle is in there), and generally providing himself with a full-service massage. Much as I was tempted to stare, I kept my eyes averted as the sound of the vibrator's motor accompanied me all the way to Tucson.

I sat, sprawled in my seat, thinking about women taking up space, drawing attention to themselves, sitting in unladylike ways, and remembering my mother's instructions. Knees together. Back upright. That was certainly never the case in my New York subway days. Or my navigating a good spot at concerts and festivals. In those halcyon days, I knew how to use my elbows to get where I wanted to go and took up all the space I needed.

I've danced to Marvin Gaye, Stevie Wonder, Gladys Knight, Hugh Masekela, Ray Charles, Mavis Staples, and the Neville Brothers in venues large and small. I've elbowed my way to the perfect spot--neither too close to the enormous stage speakers, nor too far from the dance area, becoming part of a larger organism moving together as the sounds filled us.

I still see myself whirling and looping through crowds of festivalgoers, following Sly's instructions as I "danced to the music." I danced in New Orleans, but the dance floor was in my mind's eye, and what I imagined myself doing was uninhibited, extravagant, and entirely glorious. Like it had always been. As the plane landed, returning me home, I understood that, like The Band, the New Orleans Jazz Festival had been My Last Waltz.

For younger readers, here is the cultural reference:

The Last Waltz is the film made by Martin Scorsese of The Band's lavish farewell show at San Francisco's Winterland Ballroom on Nov. 25, 1976, where they were joined by all the musical luminaries of that time.

Eight
Perched Atop the Slippery Slide

As a very old woman, I am currently perched atop a slippery slide, with each step defined by my Activities of Daily Living (ADLs). They constitute the basic activities of bathing, dressing, toileting, transfers (getting up and down), feeding, and maintaining continence. The Instrumental ADLs involve using the telephone, shopping for groceries, preparing food, keeping up with my home and laundry, driving or arranging my own transportation, managing medications, and handling money. To remain at the top and not start the slide downward to---well, you know where—I need to continue to accomplish all of them.

Let's take them one at a time. I don't take baths anymore. I used to love them, but not after getting stranded in a narrow, deep tub in Scotland while my daughter Ally, with whom I was traveling, was in the next room wearing her earphones and didn't hear my plaintive calls for help. I managed to fling first one leg and then the other to hoist myself over the tub's edge. In retrospect, it's best she never had to witness her mother in that series of naked, convoluted efforts to escape the confines of her watery prison.

Many months later, after a day or two of what I define as senior stiffness, I sprinkled a liberal amount of Epsom Salts into my apartment bathtub, lowered myself into its warm comfort, and did the secret thing I do when I'm alone and immersed in water. I sing. I'm excellent in my own mind, choosing obscure secondary show tunes and delighting myself with my Mabel Mercer terrificness. I let the Epsom Salts do their magic until the water began to cool, and it was time to return to my landlocked, non-singing life. Having learned the best escape procedure in Scotland, I navigated my way up and out, landing with a splat onto the tile floor. The black and blue marks on my behind resulted in the inevitable conclusion that my days of taking baths had now come to an unceremonious end. Now I sing in the shower, and without the constraints of a tub, I can wave my arms expressively to express the song's lyrics. I am, however, cautious about slipping, so my cabaret presentation remains stilted.

Dressing myself continues to be easily managed, although with some adaptations. The first is the circuitous way I now put my bra on, which involves connecting the hooks in the front, then sliding the entire apparatus around, and finally stuffing myself into the empty cups and my arms into the straps. However, I can't begin to get dressed too soon after a shower because if I'm still damp, the bra gets caught halfway around my body, and I can't reach the hooks to take it off or move it forward. It's just stuck there until the air dries my skin enough to tug it entirely to the bra's proper position. It comes off the same way; I first slide out of the straps, shift everything around to the front, unhook the hooks, and fling it onto the nearest surface with a relieved sigh. That's one. When I bend over to tie my shoelaces, it's best to sit down, and when putting on pants, I need to hold onto something as I slide my legs into their appropriate openings. Otherwise, dressing is still as it was in the old days.

AARP and other concerned organizations advise us, oldies, to sit on the edge of the bed for a couple of seconds before rising, use a nightlight, and avoid rugs that might cause a stumble or slippers that might do what their name implies---slip. I've heeded all of their counsel except for the slippers. I have very big feet, and the only non-slip sneakers in my size are too ugly to wear. Even at night. Even in the dark. So, I walk carefully.

My daughters insist that I wear my Apple watch at night so that if I do fall, it's programmed to call 911 if I land on the floor. I've also started doing something that old people call an anticipatory pee. It's when you're leaving the house and don't know when you'll be near a toilet, so you prepare for a future eventuality that hasn't even arisen. Even if you don't have to pee, you do it anyway. It's a senior thing. I don't even want to go into what happens when you cough. The ways those two parts of my anatomy appear to have joined forces have been an unexpected turn of events.

These days, getting in and out of a bed or a chair requires pushing down as I lift up. There was once a time I simply rose. My rising days are behind me, but I can usually get out of beds, sofas, and chairs with a good downward push. Although there is an increasing need to rock back and forth a few times while pushing before getting all the way to an upright position. I try not to make an accompanying sound, but I inevitably emit a relieved and noisy exhalation of achievement each time I succeed. My first six or eight steps after sitting or lying down are stiff and entirely ungainly, as it takes that long for whatever synovial fluid has pooled in my body to circulate again, leaving my movements more human and less robotic.

Eating has never been a problem. I have never, not once in my 87 years, forgotten to eat. Needless to say, I ate dinner later than 5:00 when I was younger, but I never forgot it entirely. I do very little cooking, but food remains a consistent pleasure. Takeout. Delivery. I make it work. It's what happens after I eat that's changed. My periodontal pockets appear to be deepening. Even with dedicated flossing using the little brushes I order by mail (utilizing the instrumental ADLs of using the computer and paying by credit card online!), food comes to rest in two precise places. I try to reshape my tongue into a sharp point to dislodge the unwanted food particle from their hiding places, but tongues don't sharpen. I'm left poking it against the trapped piece of food, hoping the contact will do the trick. It never has, but I persevere. When I'm alone, I get one of my trusty perio brushes and saw the leftover dinner out from its hiding place. But when I'm with friends, I complete the meal, accompanied by a piece of whatever the last course was.

I definitely spill more. My fine motor skills were never fabulous, but these days, food often falls from my fork or spoon onto my lap or the floor, unless I'm wearing a clean white shirt. Then it makes a beeline for my chest and splatters there. It's not just food. Keys, utensils, and pens slide out of my hands and onto the floor with increasing regularity. After spilling whatever it is, I look down accusingly at my hands and then at the object, warning them both to cut it out. No one listens.

Spilling tends to be accompanied by shaking. It's not precisely trembling, at least not yet, but it is most decidedly an unwanted movement. Especially when I'm carrying a glass of something. My floor has a trail of dribbles from the kitchen to the table. I can't get from here to there without at least a spill or two. I am going through more rolls of paper towels than I have in the past dozen years.

Nevertheless, I still shop for and prepare my meals, manage what money I have left, and do housework that doesn't involve bending down to get underneath things, over the top of things, or scrubbing the floors. I need help with that. Everything else, I manage just fine.

However, the slippery slide of my oldness is surfacing in other ways. It's not only what I can still do, but is newly accompanied by the question of why bother? I can get in and out of bed just fine, but I've begun to reconsider the notion of making the bed. Why have I spent my life making my bed every morning? In part, because there's the pleasure of easing into a bed with a smooth bottom sheet, puffed-up pillows, and a blanket that hasn't slid halfway to the floor, unceremoniously covered in whatever dust balls might reside there. It's a brief pleasure and lasts even less time than it takes to make the bed. I'm figuring out how to proceed in the mornings when I get out of bed, look back at the friendly rumpled mess, and decide whether to leave it as is. One advantage is that when I want to nap, I won't have to try to arrange myself in my reading chair or stretch out on the sofa. I can just climb into bed because it's much more inviting when rumpled. I'd be much less inclined to use it if it were carefully made.

Neither of my daughters makes their beds. My mother not only made hers but also expanded the process by adding a step, which she called dressing the bed. That involved a half dozen extra, entirely extraneous decorative pillows purposefully scattered upon the bedspread. I'm somewhere in between, but the older I get, the more I question the point.

If I stop making my bed, what else will I allow to come to an end? I worry it might become another kind of slippery slide. I already leave my dishes on the drainboard, no longer returning them to their designated place in the cabinet, concluding that it's pointless since I live alone and use the same couple of items at every meal. Having them right there on the drainboard makes everything so much more convenient.

Of course, adjustments need to be made when people visit. Unmade beds and dishes scattered around do not represent the public-facing me. That me is orderly—her home is welcoming and calm, her bed is made, and her dishes rest in their assigned places. I am not, nor have I ever been, a woman upon whom people dropped in. I don't like anything about unannounced company. I like to prepare for them, look forward to them, and then enjoy them. I never want to open my front door to see a smiling, eager face ready for a visit when I'm in chapter three of a glorious new novel. Not my, as the youngsters say, jam. Consequently, since I always know when to expect people, I can easily make the bed and put the dishes away.

My apartment has two bathrooms, and I keep the door to my bathroom closed. Any visitor who needs to use what I was trained to call the ladies' room, enters the guest bathroom and is greeted with guest towels, a charming little French jar of Q-tips, although I don't imagine anyone will be cleaning their ears while visiting me, some seashells I've accumulated, and a bud vase with some clippings from a now-dead plant. No one needs to behold the necessary pharmaceutical artifacts of maintaining my old body. They are no one's business, tucked away behind a firmly closed door. I'm shamefacedly sure that my bathroom supplies look much like theirs, and I don't know why it all feels private. If I had more years, maybe I'd reflect upon what is public and private. And most importantly.... Why? But I won't. I'm finished psychologically unearthing and improving. I simply keep the door closed. As of this 87-year-old moment, my ADLs include intermittently unmade beds, closed bathroom doors when necessary, carefully managed showers, and dish drains always ready for service.

I picture myself having spent decades painstakingly and earnestly climbing the slide, each tread a hard-won bit of awareness, insight, change, and finally acceptance until I relievedly lowered myself to a sitting position at the top, facing downward. My flesh has begun the descent, and my muscle tone, dimming eyesight, hearing, and thinning bones have all joined in. Still, I hold on to the handles at the top, facing downward, breathing the cool air, seeing the tops of the trees, hearing children's laughter, and feeling an old woman's triumph for the gifts of the climb.

Part Three
Reflections

Nine
Woman Loving Women—A History

I'm not a lesbian who fell in love with my fifth-grade gym teacher or had a crush on a junior-high classmate. One who always knew. My trajectory began later. Much later. I started my sexual life as did most white middle-class heterosexual teenage girls in the 1940s and early 50s, with the unspoken but clearly understood guidelines of sexual behavior that were codified by bases. First base was defined by the girl's mouth, neck, ears, and shoulders. Second base involved moving farther south to the border of the waist. Third base was everything short of 'going all the way.' Boys didn't have their own bases; instead, they were concerned with getting to as many of ours as possible.

Kissing simply required lips and was permissible under most circumstances. That might transition to light necking, which included the boy having the freedom to rub his hands over the clothes of the recipient, with a strong focus on the breasts. Heavy necking expanded the activity to the removal of upper garments, giving the suitor better access to the body part in question. Petting began its stealthy descent below the waist. Heavy petting was under the clothes, but not all the way. That was its own category. The longer you went with a boy, the more you allowed him to progress up to, but not including, 'going all the way.' If a girl went all the way with a boy, we believed he would lose interest in her and tell all the other boys what she had done, thus denying her the opportunity for another boyfriend for the rest of her life. Or for as long as high school lasted.

Watching 1940s gangster movies starring gun molls like Jane Greer and Lizabeth Scott, who became the enthusiastic recipients of the eventual kiss after much tough talk, led me to practice my eagerly anticipated future of kissing with my pillow. I'd lie in bed holding my pillow (representing Robert Mitchum) above my head, then slowly, very, very slowly, I'd lower it to my face, imagining our lips somehow meeting. In the movies, adults were either dramatically slow in moving their faces together or abrupt, smashing their mouths into one another. These precipitous kisses were accompanied by the woman raking her very long, pointy red nails across the man's shoulders. I understand now that it was intended to simulate extreme arousal. To me, then, it looked like a combination of smashed-up kissing as the woman scratched the man's back. Robert Mitchum sneered at his female costar triumphantly before he kissed her. Veronica Lake lowered her eyes and lifted her chin to receive her kiss. I was learning the vocabulary of how kisses were given, received, invited, and expressed.

When I was eleven, the priest at the Catholic church on the corner of our street allowed me to sit quietly in the back row while he officiated at weddings. I never told him why I wanted to be there, and perhaps he thought allowing me entry would convert me to Christianity. But faith was nowhere on my mind. I wanted to see the kiss. Every couple did it differently. Some were embarrassingly long. Some awkwardly brief. Some show-offy and others like my imaginings of what awaited me when my lips had matured sufficiently to be kissed.

That summer, I had my chance and was eager to begin. Eight of us were in Herbie's basement celebrating his birthday. After his mother had made repeated trips down the narrow stairs bearing food, then games—all embarrassingly childish ones —she mercifully gave up her blatant attempts at supervision and remained upstairs. At that point, Ernie suggested we play Spin the Bottle. I was ready. My lips were ready. And when the bottle finally pointed to me, it was Herbie himself who had spun. He would be my very first kiss. I knew this was a pivotal moment in my nearly grown-up life. Since we were all sitting on the floor, he scooted over to me, plopped his hand on my shoulder, positioned his head so our lips aligned, leaned forward, and pressed.

I didn't want to hurt his feelings on such an auspicious day by looking disappointed and a little grossed out, so when he removed his face, I smiled. Not only was kissing much less compelling than I had imagined, but I had already learned the foundational lesson that I needed to make the male kisser feel confident about his firm pressing. Even as my sexual life expanded to include going all the way, I always made sure that my male partner felt confident in his efforts. That was the girl's responsibility.

At eighteen, I married a man much older than I, entering what I imagined was a world of successful and sophisticated adults. Within the first four years, we had two daughters and a brick home in the suburbs. My days were filled with mothering, running our house, and managing our social responsibilities. Whenever my husband made a sexual overture, I responded, still entirely unfamiliar with my own desires.

As the 1950s ended, all that was required of me was to be pliant, charming, and keep most of my growing thoughts to myself. My life was carefully choreographed, and the budding thinking of young women was neither sought after nor encouraged. The constraints of being muted, except for acquiescent murmurs and smiles, left me straining at the confining borders of appropriate behavior, while just beyond my front door lay the beginnings of possibility and adventure, all of which eventually catapulted me out of my marriage and into the vibrant Greenwich Village of the mid-1960s. I initiated our divorce, imagining I had fallen in love with someone else and told myself he had fallen in love with me, not a hard leap of faith since he had said it repeatedly. But we were both already married, and after my divorce, I never saw him again.

During the years of dating that followed, I experimented with sex, with drugs, and with ever-changing political ideologies. With the beginnings of the sexual liberation movement, I was encouraged to be free of my hang-ups, my bourgeois values, and experience my sexuality as a casual and uncomplicated form of expression, which would allow me, men insisted, to free myself of the puritanical constraints that were the fundamental source of the inhibitions of earlier generations.

Sexual liberation sounded good. It seemed right. Breaking free. Expressing ourselves. I was for that. But women hadn't yet begun to talk to one another in those years. Loyalties were to 'our man', not to ourselves or each other. So many of us remained silent and tried harder to have what was defined by men as natural impulses to be sexual in ways that men preferred. White middle-class girls were not supposed to have their own hungers. Not for careers, advanced degrees, power, food, sex, or anything that would draw unwanted and fiercely judgmental attention to them. Desire itself, for anything that wasn't seen as domestic and supportive, resulted in our femaleness being compromised. Hunger and desire were for men.

By the end of the 1960s, having read the words of Kate Millet, Germaine Greer, and the Redstockings, my eyes had been opened to the idea that an underlying sexual politics was shaping the relationships between men and women. It had never occurred to me that my private sex life would lend itself to political, rather than psychological interpretation, one now shared with tens of thousands of women across the country.

I began to consider the reasons for my accommodation and yielding, why I felt my body to be in the service of the pleasure of my partner, not asking for what I wanted, not even sure what that was. With the guidance of the women theorizing second-wave feminism, I came to recognize how the sexual revolution was never about women's sexuality but about reinforcing our unquestioned availability for men. In consciousness-raising meetings, I listened to women revealing how they, too, had been criticized by men for being too emotional. Too needy. Too demanding. Too insistent. As they shared their sexual histories, I understood that I was going to have to unlearn my lessons, all the way from Herbie onward. Lessons about being responsible for the pleasures of men. Inviting men forward while receding gracefully into the role of muse or supporter. Feeling desirable as a result of being desired.

Her name was Elaine. After my divorce, I began to steer the wobbly ship of my own life. My daughters and I moved to New York City, and I got a job in a dental office in Greenwich Village. I took my egg salad sandwich and Tab to Washington Square Park every day on my lunch hour. She worked in an office nearby, and we began to spend our lunch hours together. Whenever the girl's dad took them for the weekend, we met to discuss politics, books, childhoods, dreams, and fears over coffee, dinner, and long walks through the city. As we moved into our third month of spending every free moment together, during the intermission of a mediocre play, she said, "Let's go back to my apartment and have some red velvet cake," knowing it was my favorite. What followed was a return to her place, accompanied by coffee and the cake she had purchased, a conversation that had begun to slow down for the first time, one that lengthened into an uneasy pause, which finally ended when she said firmly,

"I want to kiss you."

She didn't ask, May I kiss you? That would have required me to figure out what was happening and what I wanted to do, only to undoubtedly drown in the shoulds, the oughts, the confusion, and the doubts that would have flooded in. So, I just sat there as she got up, moved around the table, and leaned over to kiss me gently, softly, and tentatively.

"Is this ok?" she asked. "Very," I gulped, the best answer I could come up with. With that, she reached for my hand and led me into her bedroom, where, for the first time, our two bodies moved together, intensifying the two minds and hearts that had already fully opened. And I discovered that the inside of my elbow had strong erogenous properties.

During those months with Elaine, I remained astonished at how "natural" our sexual life felt to me. The voluptuous familiarity of her body was unexpectedly familiar and thrilling, but left me with new questions. Did this mean I was a lesbian? Was this relationship sufficient to change an identity I had assumed to be me all my life? Would being sexual with other women ever come close to what I was experiencing with Elaine? I realized that to answer those questions, I would have to have sex with other women—lots of them. Savoring the richness of my emergent sexuality, my curiosity and newly awakened hunger were like a live wire I sensed would permanently change everything about my life. Elaine had been a lesbian all her life, was already my wise and trusted friend, and, to my good fortune, she understood completely.

I began to frequent women's coffeehouses, bookstores, storefront art galleries, poetry readings, concerts, everywhere I thought lesbians might gather. Her name was Pat. Her name was Nancy. Her name was Cynthia. And with each woman, I began to open to myself, pleasure as the portal, connection as the landscape.

Her name was Barbara. We met in 1978 at a book party for Kathleen Barry, a lesbian-feminist sociologist who had just published "Female Sexual Slavery." There were dozens of interesting, accomplished, radical women filling her living room. While a group of us were in an animated conversation about our varied responses to Judy Chicago's Dinner Party, Barbara leaned towards me and, with an impish smile, said,

"Maria Manhattan is showing her piece that is in conversation with Chicago's. It's called The Box Lunch, designed to honor Minnie Mouse, Lucy Ricardo, Henny Youngman's wife, and Rosemary Woods. Want to go and see it?"

How could I turn down such an invitation? And that afternoon marked the beginning of ten creative and vivid years with the woman who would become my great love. Our forms of lovemaking encompassed our bodies, the torrent of words and ideas we eagerly shared, and my newly found ability, under her patient tutelage, to release my earnest self to the possibilities of play.

During those years, I was working at the Sexual Trauma Center in San Francisco, providing information, referral, and crisis counseling to women who had been brought by police to the hospital emergency room after being raped. Eyes lowered, they faced me, armed only with the police report and good intentions. Repeatedly, as they offered me the details of their rape, they disclosed an earlier violation, one where they had been sexually abused by a trusted adult. I was witnessing something for which I had no name, no words of comfort, and no training.

I tried to educate myself by reading the articles written by male psychiatrists and anthropologists, reassuring the reader that incest either happened very infrequently, or because of mothers abandoning daughters and colluding with fathers, or because girls were seductive and eager for sexual contact with their fathers. I read everything available to me, but I realized I would have to look elsewhere for my answers.

I stopped searching libraries and interviewing "experts," and instead invited and listened to women's stories. I began, woman by woman, to create small moments over a cup of tea or in a pause on a park bench where they could safely reveal their childhood abuse. It became clear to me who carried the truth about child sexual abuse. The words of those women led to the publication of "*Conspiracy of Silence: The Trauma of Incest*," published in 1978, the year I turned forty.

In 1980, the journal Sinister Wisdom was accepting submissions for a special issue titled "*The Patriarchy: Violence and Pornography*." In reading some of the submissions, I was moved by how each piece was filled with the courage of women's accounts of their histories, revealing the secrets that were the first steps towards freeing themselves from their abusive pasts. Stories like these were being told around the country as feminists created the ground upon which women might step and have the courage, safety, and affirmation to tell the truth about their lives.

I proposed adding a piece of lesbian erotica, an homage to sexual pleasure. In writing "Circling," I was able to savor the richness of lesbian sexuality in a world where the freedom to feel and express desire had been stolen from so many.

Eight years later, I published *Cancer In Two Voices*, offering our community a record of my life with Barbara facing an early death from breast cancer, and I, preparing to lose my beloved. During those years, our practices of what constituted lovemaking expanded. Smoothing cream onto the scar across her chest where her breast had been removed, first with a scented cream, then with my lips. Writing together, as she says in the film we made together, was one way we made love. Singing Broadway show tunes in enthusiastic but wavering harmony at night when she was scared or couldn't sleep. Painting the toes on her flat, wide working-class feet, nails that had never imagined polish were now fire engine red, after I soaked them in bubbles, massaged them in oil, kissed each one, then decorated them. Everything in those liminal years, from gardening to cooking, was an act of lovemaking.

Emerging from my time of mourning after her death, I returned to a life of activism. For my generation of lesbian feminists, the 80s were a time of creation and consolidation. Women were making films, writing books, opening shelters and crisis centers, theorizing a complex feminist psychology, advocating for comprehensive women's health care and reproductive rights activism, identifying the structural forms of racism, and organizing forms of resistance against their effects.

I traveled throughout the United States, Canada, Europe, and the Middle East to re-engage with lesbian feminists, some living and resisting in active war zones, and others working to build an infrastructure of information and resources for women in their communities. We gathered in storefront centers, their windows papered with fliers, announcements, and advertisements for upcoming events. The space often consisted of one large room with long folding tables, cast-off chairs from someone's living room, fluorescent lights buzzing, and the smell of stale coffee in what served as a makeshift kitchen area. We met to strategize, create the next demo, flier, press release, and action. Always, just beneath the surface of the animated conversation was the diffuse undercurrent of sexual energy, magnifying a central dimension of the aliveness and passion that fueled our work.

In the Women in Black office in Belgrade, the talk was fast, the urgency palpable, and inevitably, within those revolutionary crucibles, there was one woman whose glance held mine for an extra beat, whose fingers brushed against my arm during an animated interaction, whose words seemed to be directed towards me. The lovemaking that exploded in these brief encounters in nearby apartments was fueled by the awareness that our bodies, as well as our minds and hearts, were the sites of revolutionary and creative connection. Sevide, a poet I met during the war, whispered as we lay on her narrow mattress in a contented post-coital embrace,

"I cannot lie down with anyone who doesn't understand we are in danger."

And lie down, I did. Repeatedly. I took the excitement that fueled our activism, my body one of the many vocabularies of women loving women, into a series of brief, passionate exchanges with those who shared my commitment to creating a future of security and autonomy for women and girls.

In 1970, radical feminist Ti-Grace Atkinson wrote, "Feminism is the theory, Lesbianism is the practice." A decade later, poet and theorist Adrienne Rich broadened the meaning of "lesbian," by suggesting a "lesbian continuum" that defined lesbians as women for whom "women provided the ongoing fascination and sustenance of life." Yes. That was me. Women have been at the heart of my life, upon and within my flesh, and at the center of my thoughts, providing the ongoing fascination and sustenance of my life for the past fifty-five years.

A lesbian is a woman who sexually desires women. Check. A feminist is a woman who works to create a world where all women can live with a sense of safety and possibility. Check. A lesbian is a woman who values, admires, respects, encourages, and supports women. Check. A feminist is a woman who challenges the structures of domination that limit women's lives and opportunities. Check. A lesbian-feminist is a woman who lives a life that has been populated primarily by women, whose political activism has been shaped by work to create women-centered spaces, who writes, paints, makes music and all forms of cultural representations that center women's lives, who resists politically in the public world and personally in the domestic one, who critiques and dances, demonstrates and make loves, says no when necessary and yes whenever possible. Check. Check. Check.

These days, I continue to identify as old, Jewish, and Queer, the last a nod to changing language and theorizing, wanting to maintain my alliance with the larger community of gender-shifting folks, even as I privately continue to think of myself as a feminist whose lesbian self is still as vital and alive as when I first emerged from Elaine's bedroom.

Now, at 87, my Jewish and lesbian identities form a distinctive braid, inextricably woven into my life experiences, inseparable from one another, creating their own unique shape. Like the Shabbat challah, they have become plaited together, skillful, seasoned, and, as all good challahs should be—tasty.

Ten
Becoming a Jew in America

It's Friday night again. The weeks seem to pass more quickly now. I put on my white blouse, the one I always wear on Shabbat, and light the candles. There are dozens of Zoom services across the country that I could attend, and congregations that have created electronic communities since the COVID pandemic, but tonight, I'm choosing to write. I settle into my recliner; the only sources of light are the flickering candles and this computer screen as I try to make my way back to how and why my Jewish-American life has taken its current form.

When I reflect on my first decade, what I remember most are the rules. Rules about how to dress, rules for table manners, rules for speaking in the correct tone of voice, and rules for behavior. I was being trained for success as a well-behaved middle-class Jewish-American girl, living in a newly middle-class nuclear family, in a newly built brick house, lining the freshly paved streets.. My parents had both been raised in families that struggled to keep afloat from month to month, and they were proud to have their own three-bedroom, two-bath home, one they bought in 1940 for $9,700. This represented the beginning of their future, one in which they would become successful Americans who happened to be Jews, no longer poor Jewish kids.

I learned the barest outlines of our family history through the stories of my grandparents, stories designed to teach the values of hard work, thrift, and courage. They always centered on how, long ago, Jews lived in shtetls but were able to leave after carefully saving their money and traveling to America on ships. They worked hard and brought over all the rest of the family, or, at least, as many as they could, people who were called *greenhorns* and slept on the sofas of their families until they got a job and their own place to live.

There were always people sleeping on the living room sofas when my parents were children. Once, terrified men and women hiding from the Nazis with assumed identities were now not-quite Americans who spoke with an accent, ate unfamiliar food, and huddled together in neighborhoods that consoled and reminded them where they were from.

Yet even as Jews were being massacred in Europe, being Jewish in America meant being cosseted by protective silences. I didn't know the history that was being made in those years. I was the eldest and the only daughter of a mother who had absorbed the American dream that one can invent and remake oneself with sheer acts of will and determined forgetting.

When I was ten years old, the Jews were given a state. It was empty and mostly desert, and after everything we, as a people, had gone through throughout the centuries, this land, Eretz Yisrael, would represent the beginning of a triumphant and glorious chapter in Jewish history. That was what I was taught by my parents, by the conservative synagogue we attended only on the high holidays, and by being given the repeated opportunity to reverently slide quarters into slots in cardboard folders that would add up to enough money to plant olive trees in the empty landscape we/the Jews, were bringing to life.

My parents' hunger to be successful Americans was defined in their oft-repeated language of moving forward, not backward. Forward defined what we ate. Roast beef, not mackerel. Lamb chops, not kasha. Tea in cups, not glasses. Tablecloths of linen, not oilcloth. They were careful to have no slippage—nothing of the old ways.

In both of my grandmothers' apartment houses, the lobbies were filled with the smells of browning onions, baking pies, simmering stews, and soups from all the kitchens above the central stairwell, the odors blending in welcome—food: a vocabulary of love. But for my mother, the value and pride in having a private home was that she no longer had to smell other people's kitchens. There was always an open bottle of Air Wick on the windowsill to absorb cooking odors, and the windows were opened to "air out" the room after our meals. Having a kitchen that retained the odors of our meals was going backward. She was going forward.

My brother was to have a bar mitzvah, although I was a better student. Girls didn't have bar mitzvahs. They were confirmed, which meant a graduation ceremony after a year of Sunday school, which I attended on Saturdays, learning the carefully homogenized stories about the valor, wisdom, and holidays of the Jews.

I was learning my lessons about being Jewish and American; I lived in the greatest country in the world, where everything was possible. I would grow up and live in a Jewish neighborhood, marry a Jewish boy who was going somewhere—ideally, somewhere he could make a good living—and have children who would live a Jewish life. While being Jewish was simply an unquestioned given, the task was to become the right kind of Jewish. Not a commie or a slumlord, not a gambler or someone who did anything to go "backward" or bring a bad name to the Jewish people. Those early instructions were vague but bewilderingly covered everything. I was to be Jewish, but not in a way that was too Jewish.

At eighteen, I married a nice Jewish boy. Except that he was a man, eighteen years older than I, had been married before, lived in New York City, and had a daughter. He seemed so experienced to my undeveloped self, and after reading Marjorie Morningstar—the story of a middle-class suburban Jewish girl who breaks her parents' hearts by falling in love with an artist—ignited my dreams of doing the same. While he was a businessman, not an artist, he represented a way forward that seemed thrillingly sophisticated and mature.

The Shabbat candles have guttered out, and I reach over to turn on the lamp beside me, walk across the apartment to the closet in the back of my office, and in a pile under the summer blankets, I retrieve my 1956 wedding album. I return to my perch and open the book across my lap, trying to remember the self I was on that day.

The pictures are formulaic. There is the first dance, the carefully catered meal, the two of us feeding one another pieces of the wedding cake, the proud family, or at least, for the sake of the permanent images, required to look proud. I was fulfilling the steps of the appropriate ritual needed to take me across the threshold into my adult life and what came next— no longer a chafing, restless daughter but a wife, someone with a husband in a big city, a woman on her own. Perhaps that was why I was smiling. The ceremony itself required all the rule-bound behavior I was already well-schooled in, and I went through the required moves as taught. When this was over, I would be a married woman.

After our second daughter was born, my husband was, I understand now, eager to prove himself to his demanding, old-school father. He bought a fourteen-room English Tudor home in an upscale suburb of New York (he handled the finances, of course) that had been owned by his successful uncle. I was again back in the suburbs, only now in a bigger house than the one I had grown up in, one with a guest bedroom, master bedroom, separate rooms for each of my daughters, a living room, a den, a study- rooms to be filled with belongings to be displayed, to be cleaned, rooms to define and confine my life, decorated with my mother's eager and enthusiastic participation until everything was filled. There was no space for another chair, sofa, or vase of freshly cut flowers from our garden. The house had triumphed, and I walked among its rooms feeling as empty and unused as it was.

An inevitable divorce became final when I was twenty-seven, and our daughters were five and seven. The three of us moved from our upper-middle-class home to a small, dark apartment in New York City, which was quickly filled with my worries. Worries about finding work, about stretching the food budget, and guilt about the possibility that I had made a terrible mistake and was ruining my daughters' lives.

I found my first job in a neighborhood dental office and felt a mix of terror, relief, and pride in my hard-won, high-priced independence. Everyone in my family worried that something was wrong with me. I was a divorced woman with two children, and in 1963, Jewish women didn't neglect their children by putting their own lives first. Our lives were not mirrored anywhere in the Jewish world in which I had been raised. There, wives stayed at home to care for their husbands and raise their children, as my mother and her mother had done before her.

I close the wedding album, remembering how young I was then, how little I understood, and how unformed my own hunger, desires, and yearnings were. How hard I tried to fit in and be like everyone else. Or at least what I imagined everybody else was like.

By 1965, the civil rights movement had gathered momentum. In New York City, the local expression was a sharply polarized busing struggle for integrated schools. I became involved in our Greenwich Village school's PTA, my workdays now extending to evening meetings during which heated and often bitter arguments about the merits of busing Black children out of their neighborhood schools into primarily white communities were aired. Feelings ran high, dividing the city almost evenly along racial lines. I joined the Harlem Parents Committee in an attempt to support the painful, complex, and ultimately unsuccessful effort to integrate our neighborhood school system. We marched. We picketed. We held press conferences. We tried to counteract the public perception that pro-busing parents were all Black. I was one of the few non-Black mothers on the picket lines that ringed the school.

All of the white women were Jews. They were the kind of women I had been warned to keep away from. The wrong kind of Jews. The ones who were impolite and not worried about how others saw them, who were insistent, who raised their voices in public, who were outraged and passionate about injustice.

My daughters and I joined the first demonstration against the war in Vietnam. As we marched down Fifth Avenue 300 strong, they kept their eyes straight ahead, pretending to be oblivious to the eggs, red paint, and jeers flung at us, both proud and frightened, their pride all I noticed. When Janaea, my eldest, was nine years old, she sold Vietnam moratorium buttons in Washington Square Park, her jaw thrust forward with the urgency and importance of her task. Within weeks, she announced that she would no longer salute the flag during homeroom period since the pledge was not the truth. There was no freedom and justice, she insisted, and until there was, she would not participate. Her teacher tried to persuade my stubborn child to change her mind, but she would only agree to stand silently alongside her class and keep her hands at her sides. Freedom and justice were becoming daily words in our lives—daily Jewish words. I was learning that being a good Jewish mother meant speaking up and opening my big mouth. A good Jewish mother taught her daughters to stand up for themselves.

In what little time was left of my evenings and weekends, I volunteered at the Urban League, playing the part of a wife in a white couple looking for an apartment, one that, when a Black couple tried to rent it, was suddenly taken off the market. More meetings followed, with picket lines increasingly the outcome. Several nights a week, my young daughters would fall asleep on hard, folding chairs in church basements or across piles of coats thrown over the beds of crowded apartments. More and more often, they did their homework on the kitchen table of a stranger's apartment, trying to concentrate over the din of heated debate in the next room.

When the first pamphlets and mimeographed articles about women's liberation began circulating, I read them with hesitancy and a sense of unease. Didn't I have the "feeling with no name"? Didn't I feel uneasy reading descriptions of my life by male novelists in which I couldn't recognize myself? Wasn't I silent, silenced, and anxious to please, notwithstanding my transformation from dutiful daughter to dutiful wife to dutiful mother to dutiful political comrade?

When Janaea brought home a flier advertising a consciousness-raising meeting near our apartment and encouraged me to attend, I uneasily yielded to her enthusiasm. I considered myself a radical, someone who understood that there certainly was a 'woman' question, but that the daily realities of my life were a distraction from the more urgent struggles of the people. Once there was economic and racial parity, the military-industrial complex was tamed, and the war in Vietnam ended, then, as a woman, I might turn my attention to my own life. I had spent the past years doing what my grandmother called "sticking up for everybody" without ever noticing that my own experiences as a woman were still buried within me. Was there something to this idea that women's lives were, simply because we were women, political? I decided to see for myself.

I entered a small living room, filled with a circle of mismatched chairs and cushions. In all my hundreds of political meetings, I had never before sat in a circle with other solemn women, some meeting my gaze, others with eyes darting anxiously around the room or fastened firmly on their laps. I felt exposed and awkward in this unfamiliar environment when the facilitator asked us to say something about ourselves and why we were there. My only experience with political meetings was that the leader prepared an agenda, assigned tasks, re-established the pecking order, and women went into the kitchen to prepare food or into the back room to mimeograph flyers. No one had ever asked me to say anything about myself. What was there to say? Did they want to know my political credentials? My ideas about the woman question?

There were nine of us in that circle, in a dingy room with little light, thick smoke, and faded cotton carpeting worn thin, covered with large pillows. Each woman spoke haltingly, and I sensed no one would be interrupted, challenged, questioned, or evaluated. As the conversation developed at this meeting and all those that followed, I began to recognize some of the limitations, proscriptions, and diminishments that characterized many of my early lessons about being not only a woman, but a Jewish woman. Instructions that had been everywhere; in my home, on the radio, from the comedians' ridiculing mothers-in-law, princesses, avaricious women, in the teachings of the synagogue, in the assumptions of what was beautiful and what was entirely "too much." Too loud. Too insistent. Too demanding. There had been a correct way to be a Jewish woman: to emulate well-behaved blond non-Jewish women. Speaking mildly and not raising your voice. Never ever raising your voice.

These were not the meetings I had become used to. I had a voice here. I would be a part of how feminist political activism would take shape. I had a politics that was about my life as a woman, one that encompassed all of who I was. There would be no going backward.

I'm tired now, and as I turn off the light, close the computer, and prepare for bed, I decide that my Shabbat practice tomorrow will be to continue this excavation. Not the Torah parsha recounting the history of the Jews this week, but the Jewish history of me.

The next morning, I return my wedding album to the closet and retrieve two pictures of the woman I fell in love with in 1977, a woman with whom I spent the next decade. One is a before image, and the other an after image. The before snapshot shows us celebrating my 45th and her 40th birthdays at an extravagant party given by one of our friends, confident that a glorious future stretched out ahead of us. The after image is of our commitment ceremony, surrounded by our friendship circle, each of whom blessed us as that future, after a terminal breast cancer diagnosis, grew ever closer.

Barbara was a scholar and academic who grew up in a Jewish, socialist, working-class family. For me, Judaism served as the framework for my activism, centered on the teachings of Tikkun Olam, the moral necessity to leave the world better than I found it. But now, facing her death, we both longed for solace and ritual as we navigated this devastating reality. We were living in San Francisco when one of the first gay and lesbian synagogues in the country was being formed. Those were the years of the AIDS epidemic, and she and I were living near the Castro neighborhood, a small, contained village in the midst of the city where death had taken hold.

The first time we tentatively walked onto the basketball court of the Jewish Community Center, we saw several dozen rows of folding chairs set up facing the hoop under which the rabbi was to lead services. Each seat was filled with men, their bodies ravaged by the early HIV drugs then available, sometimes fruitlessly, in the desperate hope of sustaining their lives for just a bit longer. The rabbi, himself a young gay man, had created an enclave for men who were outside mainstream life and facing realities not yet welcome or even identified in conventional congregations.

Most of them were more knowledgeable about Judaism than we were, many from Orthodox families who had exiled them when they came out as gay. While the service was unfamiliar to both of us at first, over the next weeks and months, we felt the comfort and a sense of connection with men in varying stages of AIDS, some surrounded by family members, others with friends, men who were welcoming, recognizing Barbara's baldness as the signifier of her illness.

They always acknowledged our presence with a warm greeting, letting us know we were part of their *mishpocha,* their Jewish chosen family.

During her final months, our attendance at weekly Shabbat services, meetings with the rabbi, and planning for Barbara's funeral, both of us feeling held in this webbing of our tradition and the innovation of this gay and lesbian community taking shape around us, provided the foundation that held and steadied us.

After her death, leaving me a 50-year-old widow, I entered the mourning period, held in the reassuring embrace of a Jewish scaffolding that was thousands of years old. First, the *shiva* (the seven days of mourning), as I sat vacant and numb in our living room, filling each day with friends bringing food, memories, and the necessary *minyan* (the quorum of ten Jewish adults required for communal Jewish prayers), for a daily service, then emptying again, only to refill each day for the next week.

At the end of the shiva period, I continued through the thirty days of *shloshim* (the secondary period of 30 days) by returning to some of my ordinary life routines. Over the months that followed, I found my hesitant and melancholy way forward without her, held by the practices of my people. I was now a practicing Jew, and my first practice was to mourn.

That same year, Women in Black was established in Israel. Several months after the beginning of the first Palestinian *intifada*, a group of Israeli Jewish women began to hold silent protests in busy areas of Jerusalem in protest against the Israeli Occupation of the West Bank and the Gaza Strip. They wore black as a symbol of sorrow for all the victims of this undeclared war and carried placards with slogans urging passers-by to "Stop the Occupation." Within months, forty Women in Black groups had been formed throughout Israel, including several mixed groups of Jewish Israeli and Palestinian/Israeli women.

Bay Area Women in Black was formed following months of meetings and discussions about the need to establish a local chapter in solidarity with Israeli Women in Black, while also focusing our resistance on specific forms emerging from our Jewish lesbian identities. It was the bombing of the World Trade Center in September of 2001 that led to the creation of our first public action. Our fledgling group of performers, artists, rabbis, writers, musicians, and activists designed a community ritual at the water's edge in Berkeley, one that we very much needed for ourselves.

The gathering was created as a way to honor the dead in New York, Pennsylvania, and Washington and as a reaffirmation of our commitment to seeking justice, a central tenet of Jewish practice. *Tzedek, Tzedek, Tirdof* (Justice, Justice you shall pursue). The organizing ceremony was *Tashlich, a* ceremony performed on the afternoon of the first day of Rosh Hashanah. The *kavannah* (intention) is to identify an aspect of our behavior we want to tashlich (cast off) in the coming year and throw it, in the form of a small piece of bread, into a moving body of water. Our fear. Our cynicism. Our passivity. Our despair.

These were lesbian feminists who excelled in creating performances. There were sound checks, carefully rehearsed choreography, the preparation of baskets of breadcrumbs, creating signage, ensuring the media were present, and providing the event with good photo opportunities. All filled our focused days before the gathering by the water's edge in Emeryville, as we moved through the steps necessary to create a powerful public ritual.

At the appointed hour, we saw women, dozens then hundreds, coming over the hill and down into the grassy area where we were standing, offering a silent visual tableau of mourning. As they rounded the crest of the hill and saw us, their conversations stopped. They moved towards our makeshift stage and slowly took their seats, on chairs for those who needed them and on the grass for everyone else. A hush lengthened before the first singer stepped up to the microphone and began a *niggun*, a wordless melody. What followed was a carefully crafted program of song, drumming, poetry, and prayer. The world outside stilled, other than the birds that joined us and the faint hum of the freeway on the other side of the hill.

At the ceremony's conclusion, women were invited to take a few minutes to reflect on what they wanted to cast off in this moment of tragedy and recommitment. After a long silence, they began to rise and approach the women lined up by the edge of the water, holding baskets filled with breadcrumbs and moving to a space where they could be alone with their thoughts before throwing the bread into the moving body of water. We maintained a muted drumming, echoing the heartbeat of all those who were lost in our personal lives, as well as those who recently died on September 11th. A performer sang the same niggun with which we began as the women returned silently from the water and moved back up the hill into their New Year.

Later that year, we created a Hanukkah ritual in a synagogue where we theatricalized the politics of the Maccabees, highlighting the scarcity of oil due to those who controlled the supply. In the spring, we led seders filled with stories of refugees crossing all the Red Seas of their lives, struggling with their plagues and Pharaohs. Every Saturday morning, we stood together at street corner vigils with costumes and signs acknowledging the struggles of the Palestinian people, the Iraqi people, and the Afghan people. *Mothers Are Mourning in Israel and Palestine*, our signs read. *How Many Dead Children? Not In Our Name. Jewish Women for Peace.* We held carefully written one-pagers that we thrust through the car windows and into the hands of drivers stopped at red lights.

In 2008, after a series of trips I had taken to Israel and Palestine as a member of Women in Black, I wrote an article to convey the richness of our international lesbian-feminist activism, as well as the daily lives of both those who resisted and those who were targeted. I recently re-read the article, and my heart ached to recognize that these words, written almost twenty years ago, are equally relevant and urgent now. This is an excerpt from that piece.

Many American Jews condemn me as a self-hating Jew, and secular left-wing activists with whom I often find common cause incorporate anti-Semitic language and interpretations into their rhetoric, blurring the Israeli army and government with the Israeli people, and even virulently, with Jews around the world.

Before my first trip to this haunted country in 1999, I believed that there were parallel narratives, an equally urgent Israeli and Palestinian history, that there were real dangers Israel had to protect against, that the state of Israel was a refuge for persecuted and tormented remnants of a vibrant world of European Jews after World War II, that Palestinians had been displaced. Still, there were real possibilities for a two-state solution.

I recently returned from several weeks in Israel/Palestine, where I attended the 13th International Women in Black Conference on Resisting War and Occupation. We gathered, 700 strong, to vigil, to teach and study together, to extract from our many struggles in countries around the world the lessons of peace-making and non-violent struggle against all forms of militarism and nationalism. While my trip provided only a snapshot of the constantly changing realities that both Israelis and Palestinians face, my eyes and my heart were filled with an altered reality, requiring me to dismantle my remaining protective stories and see clearly what is.

I saw a series of concrete barriers separating people from the land, past from future, a blank, impassive wall straddling two worlds, the wounds of people echoing and magnifying one another. I saw violence done to the soil and the people as the knifepoint edge of the ubiquitous bulldozer slices through land that has been at rest for centuries, carving up the ancestors and their memories. I saw Israeli soldiers guarding one small Israeli house on a naked hillside surrounded by Palestinian villages in preparation for the expansion of Israeli settlements. I saw a concrete wall that divided a main street in a Palestinian town in half so that Israeli traffic could run more smoothly. I heard an Israeli who, when asked to move his car from the center of a narrow street in a Palestinian neighborhood in the Old City, replied contemptuously, "Why should I move my car? It's my street."

I saw Palestinian men and women walking along a dirt path to a checkpoint, vulnerable to the whims of the young Israeli soldiers on duty. I smelled the tear gas thrown at Palestinian villagers at the end of a demonstration after the internationals had returned to the safety of their buses. I watched the smiling face of the young Palestinian woman, whose house was to be demolished that week, offer us sugar pita bread as a gesture of gratitude for our concern about her life and the future of her neighbors. I saw the fury on the face of an Israeli settler as Israeli, Palestinian, and international demonstrators stood at the entrance to the settlement of Ariel, his face clenched as he slammed on his brakes and flew out of the car to snatch the Palestinian flag from the hands of a local Palestinian activist. I watched as several police officers tried to subdue him.

And repeatedly, I saw the steady, determined faces of villagers, activists, and internationals, many of whom have lived through two periods of intifada, the Palestinian protests against the Israeli Occupation of the West Bank, Gaza, and

East Jerusalem. These are the women and men who live their politics day after day, facing heartbreaking losses and occasional small successes.

At the Conference, there were visible and invisible walls that had the potential to divide women from one another—those who wanted to engage in demonstrations and those with worries about personal safety. There were women whose focus was on issues relevant to the Israel-Palestine conflict, as well as women from around the world with diverse and wide-ranging issues. There were secular and religious Jews, conservative and radical Palestinians. Women who insisted upon lesbian visibility and those who wanted to honor and respect the slowly changing conservative Palestinian cultural norms. Complexity and paradox all scrambled together. Yet in Jerusalem, a city of so many overlapping loyalties and priorities, the walls dividing us fell as we sat in overheated and overcrowded rooms to listen to one another.

In the lesbian caucus, each woman's perspective was respected and given space. There was no cross-talk, arguments, interruptions, or criticism. Every conversation was intricate, touching deep chords in women's histories and lives. There was great freedom in the way we listened, in the respect for multiple locations and ideas, patience with inexperience, and delight in welcoming newcomers to international concerns. I stretched for the best in myself as I sat in circle after circle of women—from the former Yugoslavia, Italy, Britain, Palestine, Israel, Colombia, Guatemala, and the U.S—and together, we found our way through the thickets of identity, solidarity, nationalisms, and feminist theory.

We joined Palestinian, Israeli, and international activists to sing songs of liberation in Bi'lin, a besieged Palestinian village whose land was being confiscated for the expansion of the adjoining settlement. We stood in silence before the concrete wall that bisected history and geography, facing the armed and jittery Israeli soldiers, our voices rising into the air over the rooftops of homes about to be demolished. Beside us stood the children of the village, smiling, making peace signs, and using their only English phrase, "What is your name?"

We stood, hundreds strong, lining both sides of the Kalandia checkpoint as thousands of Palestinians moved between us, necessary papers in hand. Some met our eyes and nodded; others simply moved through the familiar, dusty corridor of fence-lined passage. I joined international activists at the entrance to an Israeli settlement, led by a local Palestinian woman, proudly holding her national flag, nearly enveloped by Israeli soldiers and a cluster of armored vehicles there to protect us from the settlers. We stood in the fierce noonday sun, eyes straight ahead as the cars streamed past us, drivers and passengers cursing, waving their fists, bewildered children peering out through the windows of their parents' cars.

In Palestine, standing before a demolished house, a carcass of concrete and rubble, I recited the Kaddish, the Jewish prayer for the dead.

I was practicing a Judaism that had undergone profound changes while I was focused on political activism. There were no longer the three conventional forms of worship from my childhood. Now, along with Orthodox, Conservative, and Reform practices, there was Humanist, Reconstructionist, and Renewal Judaism. I was eager to find a path that would allow me to incorporate the practices of my ancestors, the ones my parents had shunned, a way into the tradition that would include all of me. Could I become a politically radical, lesbian-feminist Jew? I deepened my practice and began reading, studying, attending services, and finding my way both forward and backward.

Over the next decade, I read the Torah portion each week, parsing it for meaning, history, interpretations, and relevance to my life. There are five large binders in my office, each labeled with the name of one of the books of the Torah. Genesis. Exodus. Leviticus. Numbers. Deuteronomy. Each is divided into weekly sections containing my notes from years of reading, sermons, discussions, and study. Janaea told me it would be the most precious part of her inheritance.

While I knew that the Torah was the written record of a patriarchal period in history, reflecting those values, understandings, and behaviors, I was indebted to the feminist scholars who had begun to add the richness of women's prayers, music, and interpretations to the services. Two of my initial teachers were Lynn Gottlieb and Amy Eilberg, the first Reform and Conservative women rabbis in the United States. In my Renewal synagogue, we danced when welcoming in the Sabbath Bride on Friday nights. While reciting the traditional healing prayer, the entire congregation formed a circle. Those in need of healing entered the circle as we chanted *"El Na Refa Na La"* (Please God, Heal Her), the words attributed to Moses when his sister Miriam was ill. The circle was held until everyone who needed to receive our blessings had done so. Then we added the names of those who were not with us to whom we wanted to send healing. Before reciting the *Kaddish*, the prayer for the dead that concludes every service, congregants were invited to name the person they were mourning and then share a few words about them. We mourned our family members, our friends, and in an ever-widening circle, those around the world who had died as a result of injustice. The gatherings were vivid, heart-opening, and deeply rooted in the beauty and wisdom of our past, as well as the creativity and exuberance of the present.

"How can you do that?" my mother asked when I described a feminist *Yizkor* service (honoring the memories of those who had died, a traditional part of the Yom Kippur service) that ten of my women friends had created and observed together.

"You just can't make things up. Things are supposed to be the way they're written and have been done for centuries. You just can't call yourself a Jew and make it up. There is a right way to do things. An appropriate way."

Appropriate described everything when I was a Jewish girl in the America of the 1940s. There were appropriate ways to sit, eat, talk, dress, make decisions, and live as a woman in the world. Appropriate ways even to pray. No longer. Judaism is alive and being constantly renewed. I am filled with the rich solidity of thousands of years of architecture that has sustained and engaged my people. I am exhilarated by the creation of new forms of worship as well as the incorporation of Jewish practices from around the world, building a legacy that will expand for the generations that follow ours.

It is nearly dusk, and I've been typing these words all day. Still, there is one more reality I need to add.

My political life over the past fifty years has been marked by confronting and resisting injustice wherever it existed, as best I could. I know now that the country the Jews were given, the country that was the recipient of my quarters and my optimism, hadn't been, as I had been taught, ever empty of life, culture, history, or generations of Palestinian people. The current policies and the actions of the state of Israel do not represent our tradition's teachings as I have come to understand them, and the alienation I feel is profound. While Israel's beginnings are varied and complex, the outcome of these nearly eighty years is not. The genesis of the state was peopled by idealists, colonialists, visionaries, racists, socialists, xenophobes, refugees, and dreamers. But the result has become the ongoing and catastrophic occupation and destruction of the Palestinian people and their land.

The dominant narrative American Jews hear is that of the Israeli leadership and the American Jewish establishment. However, there continue to be voices reminding us of the need for moral clarity and the courage to see what is clearly and unequivocally unfolding in Palestine. The world honors them but rarely heeds their voices. The writings of Edward Said. The teaching and journalism of Rashid Khalidi, Hanan Ashrawi, Peter Beinart, Amira Haas, and Omar El Akkad.

While I am heartened by the knowledge that millions of people around the world see the necessity for the liberation of the Palestinian people as an urgent political goal, my generation of Jewish Americans has been slower to come to this understanding. The actions of the state of Israel require American Jews to turn toward the foundational teachings of our tradition. Teachings like those of Rabbi Abraham Joshua Heschel, who reminded the devout among us, "Prayer is meaningless unless it is subversive, unless it seeks to overthrow and to ruin the pyramids of callousness, hatred, opportunism, and falsehood."

I print out these pages, offer a prayer of gratitude for the gifts of my life and those of Shabbat, turn off the light beside my chair, and go to bed.

Eleven
Enough Already

How old do I have to be before I can end my lifelong pursuit of trying to improve? Will I ever conquer, or at least befriend, my demons? Shouldn't there be a cut-off expiration date for all that anxious, energy-consuming labor? When can I let enough be simply enough? Can there still be more to unearth after I've reached the august age of 87?

I don't want to give up being my best self, which, as all the arbiters of well-being and self-affirming achievement agree, is a worthy goal. We all want to try to be our best selves, whoever she might turn out to be. I don't want to come to the end of my life having remained stuck like tires on a muddy road, going over the same ground again and again, asking the same questions, and colliding with the same answers.

I have been in psychotherapy twice. Once after the death of my mother and again after a shattering breakup. My first therapist listened well, by which I mean she didn't interrupt me with curious questions, interject enthusiastic, "say more," or take notes while I was talking. As a result, I could hear myself, with her guidance, unpacking and examining my history with my mother. She made some valuable connections, some associations I hadn't seen, but mostly left me to my own devices. Her office was professionally neutral so that I could fill it with myself. At our conclusion, the best parts of my mother and my relationship with her reside comfortably within me, and the parts I struggled with are buried along with her. The experience was a gratifying success.

My second therapist was less formal and more engaged. She was my age, both of us then in our 70s, and had a tastefully decorated office, revealing the working environment of a well-read and well-traveled woman. Our work together was an active and engaged collaboration. She was innovative, agile, and patient enough to encourage me forward as I navigated the historic reasons for my ending a significant relationship. I'm very grateful to both of them.

These immersions alerted me to the endlessly compelling specificity of the unique me and the unremarkable and inevitable nature of being a person. Loss. Death. Meaning. Connection. That's the landscape we're all trying to navigate. The Buddhists remind us that suffering is at the heart of being alive. The Jews, on the other hand, as Jews always seem to have at least one more other hand than everyone else, advise that it would be a good idea to use our time here to live in a way that leaves the world just a bit better for those who follow us. There are numerous religious, philosophical, political, and spiritual frameworks to follow. Still, in the painful moments of my life, the psychological approach was always the most compelling.

Why was I who I was? How did I grow from the rocky soil that was my beginnings? What stories and behaviors did I create to protect myself against re-experiencing those injured places of my childhood? How have I recreated them in my

adult choices? Have I papered them over or healed them —
just a little? How would I know? And on it goes. Deeper and
deeper into my suffering. My autobiography. It's a narrative
where I play the lead, and everyone else is somewhere between
a co-star and a bit player. One's self is an endlessly riveting
subject matter. Until it isn't.

My storage unit contains three bankers' boxes filled with
journals, letters, dreams, and odd, once-meaningful objects. I
think about the me who recorded her life as she lived it,
searching for clues to who she was and why, and I want to put
my arms around her. The young me, the middle-aged me,
casting around for the key to unlock all these unfathomable
mysteries that would finally free me.

Did my mother want children? She didn't and told my
father clearly and decisively when they were courting. He said
that people would think he was "funny if she didn't." Do I
think my father might have been a gay man? Probably. Did his
worldly success compensate for his choice to live a
conventional life? No. His alcoholism is proof positive of that.
Did my mother sink into a massive post-partum depression
after my birth, the first of two children she never wanted? She
did. Did we ever bond when I was an infant? We didn't.

Are those the roots of my early formative years? Or do I
need to go back to my father's childhood, being the only
successful son with two ne'er-do-well brothers? My mother's
hunger to have more education, to work in an office and have
her own desk, to leave the domestic life into which she was
raised and trained as far behind as she could, only to become

trapped in a more affluent replica of the life that echoed the one in which her mother and sister had flourished.

There are an endless number of threads to unravel. What about the me that had the advantages of whiteness, a middle-class upbringing, and good health, balanced, of course, with the gender expectations of a girl growing up in the 1940s? The goal was marriage, ideally with a skill to fall back on, just in case. The 'just in case' part wasn't articulated, but it was preparation for one's husband losing his job, or leaving, or some catastrophe requiring the wife to provide for the family. I was to be a wife, but with marketable skills in reserve. The choices were either teacher or secretary, represented in those days by women who were then called spinsters, among whose ranks I am sure were a significant number of lesbians who never intended to marry at all. At least not to a man. Being able to marry a woman was then unimaginable. The path to what was considered successful adulthood was very narrow then.

The intervening decades found me moving out of my adolescent and young adult period of wanting desperately to belong and fit in, to my later series of choices to become the best iteration of a bohemian outcast I could summon. By middle age, I was finally centered in a life as an activist, a lesbian feminist, a woman living in a world of women, who, like me, wanted to create a world that did not yet exist. One where women were safe from violence and had access to healthcare, education, and housing. We were each focused on different aspects of this world-changing project. I wrote, then taught, and then wrote some more, the role that best suited me.

Yet my efforts to become a better version of myself resurfaced after the deaths of both my parents and my brother. I was now all that was left of our family. I yearned to acquit myself in their dead eyes by becoming the person they had always hoped I'd be; less judgmental about my brother's choices, kinder and more patient with my mother's striving, less stubborn, more open-minded, echoing my father's best qualities---patterns I've been unsuccessfully trying to modify all my life. They'd never get to see the upgraded me, but I would reach for her as a way to honor them.

Those became my goals, both as a way of giving myself a second chance and succumbing to the cultural encouragement that women focus their efforts on continually improving themselves. If all we can control is ourselves, then re-invention and an enhanced future remain a continuous option.

All these decades later, I'm not much less judgmental, but I notice when I am and bat those thoughts back. Sternly. I'm less stubborn and more curious because being right no longer has the same urgency as it had when I was younger. Making mistakes, not understanding, being confused, and forgetting come with the territory in one's late 80s. I am an ongoing work in progress.

Have I peeled enough onions, explored my psyche deeply enough, read enough books, and had sufficient conversations to have fulfilled my efforts to improve? Is more emotional labor required? If so, what direction should that excavation focus on? I've concluded that I've developed as much as I'm going to. This is the best me I will ever achieve; there will be no more unpacking and investigating.

Having arrived at full-ish acceptance of my psychological self, there remains the issue of what happens next. At the end of this chapter of my life, I'm going to die. That's what's next. The work I have left to complete is confronting the end of me. It's not like I'm dying next week, but it will be soonish.

While I was paying attention to my interiority, it seemed that dying became a form of accomplishment. Like doing your taxes or learning to throw pots. There is now a goal described as a "good death." And therein lies the next self-improvement hurdle. One wants to have a "good death." It seems like a worthy ambition, but who decides what that is? Are my daughters going to assess my death after I can no longer join the conversation? Mom seemed peaceful. Mom felt anxious. Do you think Mom knew what was going on? I hate the idea that I won't be a part of the conversations that will concretize their story about Mom's death. It was mine, and I should be the one to tell it. But it doesn't work that way.

Since I moved to Tucson, my daughters have urged me to think through all the details that will, of necessity, accompany my death—the good one. I've made all the medical decisions, which are now summarized on an orange laminated sheet attached to my refrigerator door with charming Parisian magnets for EMTs who may need instructions in the event of, or the inevitability of, an emergency in the middle of the night, when most emergencies occur. Whatever takes me out, no one will ever sadly murmur; she died too young. I'm way past that marker.

Then there are the legal papers, which were also uncomplicated because I don't have much of anything, and whatever I have will be divided among my daughters. I have a list of my doctors, medications, passwords, and credit cards, as well as the intention to identify everything jumbled in boxes in my storage unit down the hall, and determine what I want done with them. And lastly, where I want to be at the moment I'm leaving and who I want to be there. My afterward is left to them. Whatever ceremonies and rituals comfort them are okay with me.

My attempts at deflection at this exhaustively pointillist set of conversations initially were,

"Let me think about it." "We'll see." And "When the time comes."

None of them worked. They were prepared to skillfully but firmly bat my hesitations away and move on to the tasks at hand. And there were so many tasks. There were papers to be reviewed, rediscussed, and notarized. There were questions to be considered. There were wishes to be expressed. Wasn't it enough that I was going to die? Why did I have to have all these conversations about it? But they persevered. What did I want?

Well, the main thing I wanted was not to die before I had a chance to create a life in Tucson. But other than that, when I am dying, do I care what music is playing, what scents are scenting, whether the window is open or closed? I'm dying, and I doubt I'm paying attention to my environment. Maybe I'd try for a couple of final words or a tender smile, but beyond that, I don't think I'll be up for much of anything except the task at hand. Yet I yield to what they need. All the details are complete now, and my wishes have been identified (John

Coltrane, eucalyptus candle, open window, friends visiting for individual goodbyes).

Then there is the last part. The final words, the deathbed whispers, the moments children wait for when the dying mother finally says what they have waited for all their lives. I'm proud of you. I love you. Even though your choices were hard for me, I see how brave you have been—something like that. Books and movies revolve around these pivotal moments that release decades of grief in the child. I always thought that was both corny and manipulative. Why wait till the very last second?

Instead, I have had a series of what they call "mom's deep talks" more frequently than they might have wanted. My preference has always been to talk through my life, and not wait till the end to murmur a declaration or two. In the past, we've talked about what it was like for them to be the daughters of a young mother trying and failing to balance her own longings and ambitions with the stable domestic life they deserved. I offered them my guilty regrets about the mistakes and wounds I had caused in those years. As they moved into middle age and I became old, they found the spaciousness within themselves to forgive me my trespasses, and I became better able to forgive myself. Mostly.

Now, accompanied by my increasing physical and mental diminishments, I try to calibrate the precarious balance between my prideful need for autonomy and lifelong vulnerable yearning for dependency. (Back to the early childhood part of my explorations.) I'm patient with my daughters' overprotectiveness. But for now, the overstuffed folder marked My Death has been filed, and I turn back to this final period of my life. It will not be examined. It will simply be lived in the best way I can.

Twelve
Coming Out Even

I've always saved my most attractive or valuable clothing for special occasions. But these days, I have fewer special occasions, and for months at a time, none at all. My closet is filled with sweaters and pants I outgrew while they awaited their moment in the sun. I once owned a glorious red silk suit that I held on to for far too long, not wearing it at gatherings I thought weren't appropriate for such a flamboyant garment, until a moment where it would have been perfect, only to dispiritedly discover the pants couldn't make their way up past my hips. I still have a pair of dressy, open-toed shoes that I haven't worn in twenty years, but have always loved them and am hoping they come back into style. I've allowed them to take up permanent residence in the far recesses of my closet, where I cede them their claimed territory.

I learned the complex vocabulary of the subtle distinctions between everyday and going-out clothes in the 1950s and have refined the changing emphasis of those rules every decade since. I'd like to be a woman who is no longer worried about that kind of foolishness, but the reality is that I have always had one or two garments interred in their plastic cleaning bag, awaiting their opportunity to shine.

These days, rather than saving my loveliest outfits for a potential upcoming event that will most likely never materialize, I have begun incorporating them into my everyday wear. There used to be an admonition given to women about always wearing clean panties (or, in other versions of the story, simply panties) in case you're in an accident. I already wear clean panties every day, but if I find myself on a gurney on the way to the hospital, I want to be wearing my dusty open-toed suede shoes, colorful Scotland tunic, flowy black pants, and the Vanity Fair underpants that are just a bit too small and pinch me in places that don't appreciate being pinched but are beautiful—no more saving the best for last. I want the objects that surround my life to come to an end when I do, which I hope is not on that gurney.

I've broken my lifelong habit of reusing the same sturdy household plates and saving my delicate dishware for parties. I neither give nor go to parties anymore. While my everyday dishes have little dings, so does my face. I can't fix my face, but I can use my china every day. It's beautiful, and my scrambled eggs will taste better on it.

I need my savings and my lifespan to come out even. Consequently, there will be no replacements or upgrades, so my belongings will conclude when I do, except for the unsettling fact that I need a new mattress. The comfortable imprint my body once left upon my current one appears to have become a ravine. I now sink deeply into its recesses and can no longer avoid the several-inch-deep truth that this mattress is beyond its last supportive leg. Mattresses are expensive and last a long time, and since I'm probably not going to last a long time, what will my children do with a half-used mattress? Until my reluctant acceptance of the fact that I appeared to be sleeping in a padded gulley, I've had little need to buy anything, neither clothes nor appliances. I suppose I could replace the Dustbuster, which no longer busts dust and lies inert in the back of my linen closet. Otherwise, I have everything I want and need. My sofa has an odd-shaped stain I can't remove, so I've turned the cushion over and pretended it wasn't there. But even with the cushion on its clean side, there is a decided dip in the sofa's shape when I lie down on it that echoes the indentation in my mattress. I put a pillow in the dip.

I worried about my car. It was as old as I am in car years, and I didn't want it to die before me. I took very tender care of my old, dented chariot and kept it spotless so that, hopefully, it would notice it was being loved. My umbrella, a bottle of water, a flashlight, and an earthquake kit were tucked neatly into the rear compartment, and a bag of emergency nuts was stored in the glove compartment. Every surface was polished, pristine, and poised for years of service.

But even with my painstaking care, some bad guys (I assume they were guys) who were not privy to my scrupulous automotive relationship stole the catalytic converter from my car. The replacement and protective shield cost more than the car was worth, and I had to resign myself to the fact that my Prius and I would not accompany one another to the end of things.

Within days, I uncharacteristically threw financial caution to the wind and concluded that I needed to have one red car in my life. All the others had been muted, dark, forgettable. It didn't matter to me what brand of red it was. Just one that I could afford. My decision was entirely predicated on the color red. The psychologists among you are free to make your own interpretations.

I'm uneasy about the longevity of my teeth. I have a bicuspid that my dentist tells me may "fragment." When I asked why and what I might do to protect it, she reassured me that it was simply because the tooth was old. Old things fragment, she repeated with what she intended to be a winning and, of course, youthful smile. So, except for an errant bicuspid, I'm counting on my teeth to remain firmly attached and neatly lined up as they accompany me to the end. Do I really want to invest my dwindling resources in costly dental work that will be hidden in the recesses of my mouth?

Several years ago, I divided up my mother's sets of dishes, the large wooden box of her sterling silver, the vases and tablecloths, wine glasses, and large serving platters — artifacts from a life I am no longer living. My daughters have all the excess I inherited from my mother's determined upward mobility. Yet it's still more than I need, requiring an ongoing process of scaling back with the intention of leaving a small footprint when I'm dead. My behavior might be described as downsizing, but that sounds too industrial-- people losing jobs, factories closing. I'm leaving a small footprint.

Having heard so many stories of beleaguered middle-aged children left to wade through cabinets of mugs with funny sayings, decades of old tax returns, an accumulation of photo albums, high school yearbooks, stacks of 78 albums, stained cookbooks, novels that were culturally relevant forty years ago, small hand-painted bowls and local tchotchkes collected during a lifetime of vacations, I want to make it simple for my daughters. While I imagine some of what they unearth may be filled with sweet memories for them, most of it won't. It will just be stuff.

I've pared everything down to the things I want around me and put everything else into bankers' boxes. Janaea and Ally have their own designated cardboard repository filled with elementary school photos, high school and college graduation satin robes, birthday cards, diplomas, letters, and whatever other ephemera have surfaced. Three boxes labeled 'Family History' contain my father's driver's license, browned photos of ancestors, and my mother's once-creamy, now cracked leather gloves. The sterling silver bell she rang when she was old, sick, and unable to call out to me. My brother's tallit (prayer shawl). My father's shoehorn with its graceful ivory handle. The home movies he made from inside the plane as it took off and landed in 1944, so proud to be among America's first air travelers. I've transferred the reels onto DVD to make it easier for my daughters to watch. I know that DVDs are no longer electronically relevant, but given what it cost me to transfer my history onto them, that's as current as they'll get.

Three boxes are all that remain of my parents' eager accumulation of belongings. Everything that filled their homes came to an end with them, leaving barely a trace. Eight decades of life packed into boxes, leaving my memories to fill the rest of the space.

I have a Sandy box filled with Mother's Day and birthday cards, letters, and pictures that trace the contours of my life. A small drawstring bag carries the key to the home I once shared with my beloved-- a red enamel doorknob, her first gift to me. I hope my daughters will cherish these precious artifacts, as I honor the history of my mother's apothecary jar and my grandmother's single lace handkerchief.

They will undoubtedly identify the specific bits and pieces they want that represent me. Neither shares my taste in art, and they don't respond to the photographic images on my walls, scenes that give me such pleasure, images of the natural world and domestic life that invite me to enter them. I imagine they'll keep some of my stuff and store some because they can't decide yet what to do with it. The rest they'll donate to an organization that can make good use of them. I gave my mother's once-elegant but outdated clothes to an organization that provided outfits for what was euphemistically called "under-resourced women newly entering the job market." None of my clothes would be suitable for a young woman starting her work life. I have a lot of out-of-style and outdated dressy and standard old-lady clothes: elasticized waistbands, loose, comfy tops, and sturdy walking shoes. I suppose Goodwill will become my closet's final resting place.

My daughters are both sentimental women, each in her own way. I trust that they will have a box or two and perhaps an old suitcase filled with my letters, pictures, and all the notes and cards I have sent them over the years. I hope they've saved at least some of them.

Janaea putters like I do, and she'll choose an object that evokes me, and every few months, will move it from surface to surface. Ally will place me somewhere where I will remain. Her environment remains constant, and whatever surface I initially land on will be where Mom is—permanently.

I expect I will end up in a carton filled with the objects they have chosen, perhaps not the ones I intended, somewhere in the recesses of a closet to be opened on my birthday or a ceremonial occasion. I'll be remembered, stories told, laughter downshifting to sighs, and then put back in the box. Mom will have come out even.

Thirteen
Considering Death: Reflections on My End

I think about my death all the time. Well, at least a couple of times a week. How will it make itself known? With a slow decline from an identifiable disease? With a sudden accident or stroke? I hate surprises. Always have. Dying in my sleep would be my preference, but I know that's only one of the ways death shows up.

When I was younger, by which I mean in my 70s, I completed all the obligatory medical and legal paperwork to clarify my wishes, had all the necessary emotional and explanatory conversations with my children, and sorted through my belongings. I figured I was ready.

Well, I'm not. My death is no longer a matter of time. The feel-good homily, encouraging oldies to live as though each day is their last, is a splendid way to keep us in the present moment. Still, I'm winding down and am reaching for a clearer sense of direction.

I subscribe to the counsel of folks who urge us to: Eat the Chocolate! Ignore the dust accumulating around the edges of the room! Live your Best Life Now! Don't kill time! Do what makes you happy! And so forth. The thing is, I'm already doing that. Well, maybe, except for the dust thing. Maternal admonitions never die. But my end is in sight, and am I supposed to wait for it while living my best life?

While I try to do that, America is coming undone, and I want to contribute my two cents to the mix of opposition springing up across the country. My two cents have been a part of American resistance movements for over fifty years, and I consider my quavering voice, diminishing hearing, and need to sit rather than march at demos as me living my good life. But it's both sad and scary as I witness institutions brought to their knees, families losing health insurance, jobs, homes, and health care, libraries and schools increasingly without the resources to educate the next generation, vulnerable Americans losing the ability to work, honor their proud identities, and build for their futures. Some days, I fear that America and I will come to an end at the same time.

I'm slowing way down. I've saved a carton of appointment books dating back to 1978, imagining I was keeping a record of my life, hoping perhaps that the date and time of events would evoke memories of the experiences. They don't. I don't even recognize some of the names of women with whom I apparently spent a good deal of time. Still, I can trace the tempo of my life through the pages of those faded accounts. I had coffee dates, meetings, lunches, errands, movies, theater, organizing, planning, demonstrations, travel, and dinners — day after exuberant, energetic day. Only in my 70s did the rhythm of those days begin to diminish-- just a bit. Now, I have transitioned from those early halcyon times to maybe one or two things a day. And that depends on the time of day, how crowded the meeting place is, how well I slept the night before, and how my oomph is doing.

This afternoon, for example, I'm having coffee with a woman who was once the theater critic in Tucson but now has Chronic Fatigue Syndrome. Her best energy is in the mid-afternoon, so we're going to visit at 3:00. But last night, I received an email from the Tucson chapter of Indivisible with an announcement that a group of Jewish activists is forming called the Oy Veys, and will hold their first organizing meeting at Revolutionary Grounds at 5:30. Right away, this signals to me that these are not oldies because that's the time of day they are getting off work. I am, on the other hand, beginning to tuck in for the evening. Even if I wasn't, two back-to-back interactions that require me to focus and be fully present, both at the end of the day, are neither appealing nor physically possible. I'll wait for the second Oy Vay meeting and keep my coffee date.

These calculations have become an integral part of daily life. My momentum is fading, as is my strength, stamina, and, sometimes, even the desire to engage. These days, I spend more of my time doing the things I've loved all my life. Reading, writing, and talking with other women about reading and writing.

Much of my work over the past few decades has been designed to break the silences that surround the lived realities of women's lives. Abortion. Sexual violence. Breast cancer. Mothering. Daughtering. Over the past dozen years, my writing has taken a more personal turn, and I have made the subject matter myself—one aging woman finding her way into a life of oldness. I'm dealing with the complicated issues of dependency, autonomy, loss of family and friends, as well as the vulnerabilities and freedoms of aging.

Still, I recognize that one subject that remains is my death. As a woman who emerged from the Our Bodies, Our Selves generation, the idea that saying our own yeses and nos, determining who enters our bodies and when, if we give birth or have abortions, and having accurate information about how to keep our bodies as healthy as possible is our birthright. And so, I have concluded, is the relationship to my death. It's my body that's coming to an end, and I want to have a say in how that happens.

I know there's no way to know what will happen in the next five minutes, let alone the next couple of years. But there is a way to think about what, if it is possible, I want for my death. Not soon. I hope not, anywhere in the near future. But the limitations of time have a way of sharpening my clarity and focus. The protections and defenses that once shielded my insecurities, wounds, and vulnerabilities have largely evaporated. What other people think about me, what it is I'm supposed to be or do, has gone the way of my once unlined face.

My ex-husband was hoping to live until 100 and made it to 99 before he died, unable to walk, see, hear, or manage any of his bodily functions. Our daughters were loving companions to him in his decline. They centered him in their busy lives for nearly six years as he became increasingly unable to be anything other than an appreciative recipient of their care and attention. It was the best of all possible endings for him, but as

I watched this slow erosion, I was clear that his choice did not make sense for me.

If it does turn out that my death is sudden, it will be hard on my daughters. It would be ideal for me, but they would do better with a slow, tender decline before I pop off. That way, they can say all the things that are important to them, things that they want me to know, and offer the small, kind acts of love—everything they did that allowed them to release their dying father.

While I know that it's impossible to plan one's end, I've done it anyway. I want to die quietly in my sleep, very far into the future—no bottle of pills on the table next to my bed. No loved ones leaning over me and sobbing. None of that. Just my usual nighttime ritual of brushing, flossing, a little lotion here and there, a book beside me, pillows fluffed up just right, I lie down, and bingo! Of course, I know better. But still.

Now, in the well-practiced move that Jews have been making for centuries, I lift my shoulders in a slight shrug and remind myself that what I want--continuing health and a friendly mind, and what I fear--the loss of democracy and falling, in that order-- have nothing to do with anything at all. It's only going to be how I manage whatever comes next. You'd think that, having faced this lesson so many times throughout my life, I'd have at least a leg up on this, accepting 'what is' business, but it doesn't seem to work that way for me. If I live a bit longer, laws may change. Or I may be hit by a bus. For now, I understand that my death will unfold as it will. My days of trying to be in charge have come to an end.

I have accompanied the deaths of my parents, my brother, a beloved, and several close friends. Each was distinct, and several were chosen. It was the San Francisco of the 1980s, during the AIDS epidemic, when young men were dying of a disease that was unrecognized by both the medical establishment and the general public. Invisible, shamed, and without resources or public acknowledgment, these men brought a sense of dignity to their deaths by choosing when and how they would take place. There was an underground then, and the necessary medications were available for men who wanted to put a ceremonial end to their suffering. We surrounded R. as his partner crushed the drugs into the Waterford crystal goblet he held up in a toast to each of us before he drank it. This scene, and others like it, were echoed throughout San Francisco and, undoubtedly, the country in those years. As my partner was dying of breast cancer, she decided that, like all of the gay men we knew and loved, she too wanted to determine when it was her time. And she did.

We wrote *Cancer in Two Voices* then, but decided to leave out that part of the story because neither of us wanted the book to become a cause célèbre about chosen death. The book was about our love, how we navigated her death, and what the experience meant to each of us, wanting it to serve as a guide for others going through a terminal illness. I was 49 years old when she died, and her decision and our years together left a deep imprint on me.

I am very grateful to have arrived at the freedom of being all the way old. Being able to speak my sense of the truth of things without hesitation. Knowing ever more clearly who this life has led me to become. And to take my leave with the values I have tried to embody over all these decades.

My life will come to a natural end, and if I can read, write, talk, and think, I'm happy with that. But there will be no surgeries or invasive medical treatments if I am diagnosed with a disease. There will be no further replacements for worn-out body parts. When my body signals it's coming to an end, I will come to an end.

I don't want to be seen as plucky. I don't want to be an exception. I want to be tender with my life, with my oldness, with my slowing down. I want to be grateful for the decades I have been given and for how I have filled them. I want to bask in my daughter's company, my deep friendships, the food, the love, the laughter, and the richness of my life. And when my physical plant grows weary, I want to release it and see what comes next. I'm a little curious about that part.

My daughters continue to watch me, just as I watched my mother. They still need me, delight in the stories, the inside jokes, the shorthand. All of our history is alive when we're together. I understand the false comfort of my written and verbal instructions, and know all too well that life may have a different future in store for me.

Beside my bed hangs a faded 3x5 card, carefully matted and framed, upon which my beloved wrote, "There is no greater gift than that of the new day." She wrote that as she was dying. I read that each morning as I am living. Because as long as I'm alive, I will be fully alive. Every single minute of my life will be on purpose.

Now, I'm going to put on my "Let This Radicalize You" tee-shirt and drive my bright red car to pick up the sign I made for this Saturday's demonstration. It says in equally bright red letters, WE THE PEOPLE. I'll take my cane that opens into a seat and find a spot in the shade, sit and hold my sign at that, and all the other gatherings that will follow. I'll continue to write, to dance until I need to sit down, to resist where resistance is required, to open my arms to what life brings, to ignore the chin hair for as long as I can before I pluck it, to continue to wonder at the rich complexities of being human, and to be tremendously grateful for every single day I still have before me.

Ever onward!

Acknowledgments

I am grateful to Frances Reid and Nan Gefen, my Bay Area writing buddies who listened, encouraged, supported, edited, and accompanied every word of these pages. Repeatedly.

Penelope Starr, my Tucson writing partner, who kept me on track and on schedule with our weekly editorial exchanges and deepening friendship.

Jan Holmgren, Sabena Stark, and Rivkah Walton, whose close reading provided invaluable feedback.

Donna Korones, whose wise counsel has accompanied my reading, my writing, and my life for thirty-five rich and sustaining years.

Robin Steinberg, whose exploration of Jewish ethics grounded me in the wisdom of Torah during this writing.

Lavina Tomer and Joyce Bolinger, for the blessings of their open hearts and community-based political activism.

To Ian Henzel and Rattling Good Yarns for shepherding our LGBTQIA+ stories into the hands of readers who are eager for them.

And, as always, to my daughters, Ally and Janaea, for gently alerting me to a detail needing inclusion or omission, for their generous willingness to have their lives made visible on the page, and for their support of my efforts to tell this part of my story.

Each of you brought a distinct sensibility, were willing to read and re-read, nudging me to jettison a draft, or try it from another angle, or be less abstract, then letting me know when I arrived at where I was trying to go. Thank you.

About the Author

Sandra Butler is a Jewish lesbian-feminist, mother, lifelong activist, and the author of six books. Each is centered on the need to document what had been considered unsayable. She has written about violence against women, death abbreviating the life of a lesbian couple, mothering middle-aged daughters, and three books spanning the decade of her eighties. Those represent the first 88 years and are captured at sandrabutler.net. What's ahead remains to be seen.